Malaysia

Front cover: Masjid Ubudiah, Kuala

Kangsar
Right: M
the Gre:

TOP 10 ATTRACTIONS

Petronas Twin Towers The world's tallest pair of buildings are a striking sight on Kuala Lumpur's skyline (page 41)

Pulau Langkawi An island of many beautiful beaches and impressive geological formations (page 67)

Melaka Explore the streets of this famous historic port city (page 91)

Pulau Sipadan This famous island in Sabah is one of the world's top dive sites (page 131)

Visiting a longhouse An experience not to be missed when travelling in the state of Sarawak (page 114)

Taman Negara A national park of ancient rainforests and river rapids (page 84)

George Town Its architecture ranges from colonial to Chinese (page 58)

Sepilok Orang-Utan Rehabilitation Sanctuary Prepares once captive and orphaned animals for life in the wild (page 129)

Kinabalu Park Superb scenery and fascinating flora and fauna make it a major attraction in Sabah (page 124)

Gunung Api's Pinnacles A mesmerising sight in Gunung Mulu National Park (page 119)

A PERFECT TOUR

Day 1 — KL

Enjoy a day in the capital, Kuala Lumpur. Catch a taxi to Chat Masala (see page 154) for breakfast in Brickfields' Little India, then head to Menara Kuala Lumpur for stunning city views. Walk to Jalan Alor for lunch. Those with stamina can head to the Hindu shrine of Batu Caves. Return downtown to the Central Market for curio shopping, and for dinner, eat your way through Petaling Street's night market.

Day 2 — Hill Stations

Take a bus to Cameron Highlands and have lunch at one of the roadside cafés. Visit the Sungai Palas Tea Centre for a factory tour. Enjoy panoramic views of the tea gardens from Tea'ria (see page 156), followed by a relaxing spa session at the Cameron Highlands Resort or a game of golf, before dinner at The Smokehouse Restaurant (see page 155).

Day 3 — Penang

After breakfast at Restoran Kumar (see page 155) transfer to Penang Island by van. Hire a taxi for the rest of the day and head to Suffolk House for a tour of Penang's first 'Great House'. Dine in the ambience of a historical home (see page 157). Work off lunch by cycling around Balik Pulau's idyllic fishing villages. Return to George Town and perhaps enjoy the nightlife at Upper Penang Road.

Days 4–5 — Perhentians

Fly to Kota Bharu and catch a taxi to Kuala Besut jetty. Set foot on the palm-fringed islands of Perhentian Kecil and Besar. After lunch, relax on the beach or scuba dive. Next day, visit the other island for snorkelling or trail hiking. Return to Kota Bharu for Kelantanese cuisine at the night market.

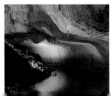

OF MALAYSIA

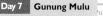

Day 7 — Gunung Mulu

Fly to the World Heritage Site of Gunung Mulu National Park and discover the canopy walkway. Explore the enormous caves before watching the famous bat exodus.

Day 9 — Padas River

Ride the North Borneo Railway from Tanjung Aru to the historic town of Beaufort. Change trains to Pangi and from there enjoy the thrills of white-water rafting this challenging river. Return to Kota Kinabalu in the evening for a late dinner at the beachside Coast Restaurant and Bar (see page 160).

Day 6 — Kota Bharu

Soak in the sights and sounds of Pasar Besar Siti Khadijah, the central market that sells everything, including brunch. Visit the War Memorial Museum or catch a performance at the Cultural Centre. Fly to KL International Airport and while waiting there for your flight to Miri, enjoy a foot massage and dinner.

Day 8 — Kota Kinabalu

Return to Miri for your flight to Kota Kinabalu. Go island-hopping at Tunku Abdul Rahman Park or visit the longhouses of the Heritage Village. After browsing the Handicraft Market by the waterfront, head up to Signal Hill Observatory for a gorgeous sunset.

CONTENTS

Features

INTRODUCTION

As Malaysia continues resolutely into the modern age, it remains, culturally and historically, a rich, multi-layered blend of traditions fuelled by a modern, busy and outward-looking economy. From sandy beaches, broad rivers and deep forests, to rising skyscrapers and wide expressways, Malaysia is set to exceed visitors' expectations.

Visitors see the traditional juxtaposed with the modern among Chinatown shophouses, in the vibrancy of night markets, and even in the modern shopping centres. They see great architectural splendour among the many mosques, Chinese and Hindu shrines, and even the Petronas Twin Towers of Kuala Lumpur. The ways of the past can be felt amid the longhouses of Sabah and Sarawak, in the kite-flying and top-spinning traditions of Kelantan and Terengganu, and in the evocative colours of batik art.

Your gateway to Malaysia will probably be through its capital, Kuala Lumpur, a prosperous and modern city where mansions, mosques and temples jostle with expressways and skyscrapers, and where parks and gardens balance the urban areas.

Facts and figures

Peninsular and East Malaysia together cover a total area of 329,759 sq km (127,317 sq miles). The peninsula is 750km (466 miles) long and about 350km (218 miles) at its widest point. It is only two-thirds the size of East Malaysia. Some four-fifths of Malaysia was originally covered by rainforest. Of the many rivers, the peninsula's longest is the Pahang, at 475km (295 miles). In East Malaysia, the longest river is the Rajang, at 563km (350 miles).

The Kuala Lumpur skyline from Kampung Baru

In the Cameron Highlands

In the heart of Southeast Asia, Malaysia is about the size of Japan and has a population of over 26 million. The country is divided into two major regions: the peninsula, bordered by Thailand, the Strait of Malacca and the South China Sea; and East Malaysia, whose two states, Sarawak and Sabah, are located on the island of Borneo, 800km (500 miles) across the South China Sea. Sarawak and Sabah are vast regions of forests, rivers and mountains bordering the Indonesian state of Kalimantan and the sultanate of Brunei. Industry and urban society are concentrated on the peninsula, especially on the west coast, while East Malaysia is dominated by rainforests. The two regions share a hot, humid climate, but differ greatly in their population density and urban development.

Malaysia's relative wealth is reflected in the excellent road and rail networks along the peninsula's west coast. Its per capita income is one of the highest in Southeast Asia.

Nature's Supremacy

Whether you are staying at a beach resort or visiting a city, a stand of forest is never far away. Even in modern, urban Kuala Lumpur, you can find a forest reserve more than a century old.

The country's prosperity has come from its coastal plains, wider on the west than the east side of the peninsula. Malaysia rose first as a trading point for Asia and Europe, with the port of Melaka (or Malacca). Then came tin mining and rubber plantations followed by palm oil, timber and petroleum and gas. Rice paddy fields in the northwest and around river deltas on the east coast, and on hillsides in Sarawak and Sabah, are where Malaysia's rice is cultivated. Mangrove swamps along the coast and nipa palms give rise to mangrove forests. The world's oldest

Five Kinds of Forest

Variations in soil, slope and altitude give rise to five kinds of forest:

Mangrove forest. Mangrove trees and shrubs grow on coastal marshland in the brackish zone between the sea and fresh water. An associated species is the low, trunkless nipa palm, whose fronds have traditionally been used as roofing material for coastal huts.

Freshwater swamp. Abundant fruit trees in the fertile alluvium of river plains attract prolific wildlife. Where swamp gives way to dry land, you may see the fascinating, monstrous strangler-figs.

Dipterocarp forest. Named after the two-winged fruit borne by many of the forest's tallest trees, this dry-land rainforest is what you will see most frequently from just above sea level up to an altitude of 900m (3,000ft).

Heath forest. Poor soil on the flat terrain leading to foothills or on sandy mountain ridges produces only low, stunted trees with thick leaves.

Montane forest. At 1,200m (4,000ft) and above in large mountain ranges, or as low as 600m (2,000ft) on small isolated mountains, the large trees and liana creepers give way to myrtle, laurel and oak trees.

rainforests engulf low but steeply rising mountain chains that cross the peninsula from east to west, with one long north–south Main Range as their backbone. Until the highway construction of the modern era, access to many forested areas had been – and sometimes still is – only by river.

In East Malaysia's states of Sarawak and Sabah, plantations alternate with marshland on the plains before giving way to the forests of the interior. To the south, a natural barrier of mountains forms the border with Indonesian Kalimantan. Near the coast at the northern end of the Crocker Range is Gunung Kinabalu (Mount Kinabalu). At 4,095m (13,435ft), it is one of the highest peaks in Southeast Asia and popular with climbers.

With the growth of tourism, resort facilities have burgeoned in islands such as Penang, Pangkor and Langkawi on the west coast of the peninsula, Tioman on the east coast, and around Sabah's islands off Kota Kinabalu.

To go to Malaysia without setting foot in the rainforest would be to overlook one of the essential features of the country. Sounds flood in from all sides: the orchestra of cicadas, the chatter of squirrels, the cries of gibbons, and the calls of hornbills. Animal life may be harder to spot as, unlike the wildlife of the African plains, most animals of the Malaysian rainforest are not conspicuous. Tigers and leopards remain rare, and the elephants, rhinos and bears are the smallest of their kind.

Many and Diverse Peoples

Malaysia can be proud of the continued coexistence of the three prominent peoples of the nation: Malays (usually Muslim), Chinese (mostly Buddhist) and Indians (mainly Hindu). Although there have been periods of social unrest in Malaysia's past, the people generally live in harmony, and it is not unusual to see a mosque, pagoda, temple and church all built close to each other. Another feature is the marvellous diversity in the nation's food, with food centres often serving

Malay, Chinese and Indian dishes at adjacent stalls. The country's multiculturalism is also apparent in tribal communities like the Kadazan/Dusun of Sabah, the Iban of Sarawak (see page 105) and the Orang Asli people who first arrived on the peninsula at least 11,000 years ago.

The Malays, or Bumiputra (meaning 'sons of the soil'), make up over half the population and this is reflected in Islam's status as the national religion, with Malay – Bahasa Malaysia – as the national language.

The bulk of Malays are humble town or village-dwelling people, tending

Mangroves in Langkawi

goats and buffalo, growing rice and working in the coconut, rubber, timber, rattan and bamboo industries. Just as court rituals are influenced by the ancient customs of pre-Muslim Malaya, so a mild Sunnite version of Islam is often seasoned with the ancient beliefs of animist medicine-men.

Religious Tolerance

To the outsider, public life in Malaysia may sometimes seem like one religious holiday after another. All the world's major beliefs, along with an array of minor ones, are practised in Malaysia. While Islam is the official religion, most other faiths are treated with a tolerance that contrasts with ethnic struggles at the political or economic level. The free pursuit of all

Useful phrases

Courtesy and knowledge of a little Bahasa Malaysia are always welcomed. A simple phrase such as *terima kasih* (thank you) is likely to be answered *sama sama* (you're welcome). Other phrases can be found in the language section (see page 171), but just remembering *selamat pagi* (good morning) or *selamat tengah hari* (good afternoon) is worth the effort.

beliefs is guaranteed by the constitution.

Islam is observed by some 60 percent of the population, mostly Malays, but also some Indians, Pakistanis and Chinese. First introduced by Arab and Indian Gujarati traders, its earliest trace is an inscribed 14th-century Terengganu stone. From 1400, the religion was spread through the peninsula by the Melaka sultanate. Today, each sultan or ruler serves as leader of the faith in his state. Since Islam makes no distinction between secular and religious spheres, it regulates many aspects of everyday life, from greeting people to washing and eating.

Now practised by 19 percent of the population, Buddhism was introduced to the peninsula by early Chinese and Indian travellers, but only took hold when Chinese traders came to Melaka in the 15th century. With their 3,500 temples, societies and community organisations, the Chinese practise the Mahayana (Greater Vehicle) form of Buddhism, which evolved in the first century BC. A more rigorous form, known as Hinayana (Lesser Vehicle), is practised by the Thais in Kelantan, Kedah, Perlis and Penang. For most Malaysian Chinese, the Confucian moral and religious system coexists with Buddhism.

As the country's earliest organised religion, pre-Islamic Hinduism of the Brahman priestly caste reinforced the authority of the Indian ruling class. Rituals of that era survive in Malay weddings and other ceremonies. Modern Hinduism in Malaysia has been shaped by 19th-century immigration from the Indian subcontinent. The largest contingent and most powerful

Malaysia is known for the heterogeneity of its ethnic profile

influence were Tamil labourers from southern India and Sri Lanka, with their devotion to Shiva. Temples have been built on almost every plantation worked by Indian labourers.

Christians make up 9 percent of Malaysia's population, mostly in Sabah and Sarawak. This is largely due to Catholic and Methodist missionary work from the 19th century onwards, although many of the Catholics are of Eurasian origin, dating back to the Portuguese colonisation of Melaka. Christmas is widely celebrated throughout the country and Easter is a public holiday in Sarawak and Sabah.

Despite its reputation for religious and multiracial harmony, Malaysia faces the challenge of maintaining stability. In the political sphere, rifts have deepened between fundamentalists and more moderate Muslims. Ethnic wealth gaps are also a problem. Nevertheless, Malaysia remains one of Southeast Asia's most successful economies, and attracts tourists with its diverse landscapes and multicultural, welcoming population.

A BRIEF HISTORY

Over the centuries, life in Malaysia has always been able to attract incomers. Bountiful food sources may have made it an inviting place to settle. In Perak's Lenggong Valley, archaeologists have revealed the site of the earliest civilisation in the country with the discovery of a stone hand-axe 1.8 million years old. Over in Borneo, the oldest human settlement is the Mansuli Valley in Sabah's east coast Lahad Datu district, where more than 1,000 stone tools dating back 235,000 years have been discovered.

By 2,000 BC, the nomadic Orang Asli people, hunting with bows and arrows, were driven back from the coasts by waves of immigrants arriving in outrigger canoes. Mongolians from South China and Polynesian and Malay peoples from the Philippines and the Indonesian islands settled along the rivers of the peninsula and northern Borneo. They practised a slash-and-burn agriculture of yams and millet, exhausting the soil and imposing a semi-nomadic existence from one forest clearing to another. Families lived in wooden longhouses like those still seen among the Ibans of Sarawak. Other migrants arrived and settled along the coasts – sailors, fishermen, traders and pirates – known euphemistically as *Orang Laut* (sea people).

The Indian era

Between the 7th and 12th centuries AD and before the arrival of Islam, Buddhism, Hinduism and South Indian culture and language flourished in Kedah and the coasts of Borneo, which were then under the Srivijaya Empire. With its base in Sumatra, Srivijaya controlled the Strait of Malacca, a key link between the Indian Ocean and the South China Sea. The Malay language was introduced – many Malay words are derived from Sanskrit and Tamil, and some Malay social customs, especially wedding rites, reflect Hindu customs. (Malayu was also the name of a Sumatran state). What is now the state of Kedah benefited from the plough and other Indian farming practices. During the golden era, *candi* (Hindu temples) were built in Bujang Valley at the foothills of Gunung Jerai in Kedah and on Borneo, at Santubong.

As Srivijaya declined in the 14th century, the Malay peninsula was carved up among Siam (now Thailand), Cambodia and the Javanese Hindu empire of Majapahit. Around 1400, fighting over the island of Singapore drove the Srivijaya prince Parameswara to seek refuge up the coast of the peninsula in Malacca (now known as Melaka).

Working in a rice paddy field

The glory of Melaka

The Chinese were the first to spot the strategic and commercial potential of Melaka – once an infertile, swampy plain – as a harbour sheltered from the monsoons, with a deep-water channel close to the coast. In 1409, under a directive from Emperor Chu Ti to pursue trade in the South Seas and Indian Ocean, a Chinese fleet headed by Admiral Cheng Ho called into Melaka. They made Parameswara an offer he could not refuse: port facilities and financial support in exchange for Chinese

Melaka was once a busy trading port

protection against the Siamese (Thais). In 1411, Parameswara took the money to Beijing himself, and the emperor gratefully made him a vassal king.

Twenty years later, however, the Chinese withdrew. The new ruler of Melaka, Sri Maharajah, had switched his allegiance to Muslim traders. Islam won its place in Malaya not by conquest but by trade and peaceful preaching. Bengalis had already brought the faith to the east coast. In Melaka, and throughout the peninsula, Islam thrived as a strong, male-dominated religion, offering dynamic leadership and preaching brotherhood and self-reliance – all qualities ideally suited to the coastal trade. At the same time, Sufi mystics synthesised Islamic teaching with local Malay traditions of animistic magic and charisma, though Islam did not become the state religion until Muzaffar Shah became sultan of Melaka (1446–59).

Yet the key figure in the sultanate was Tun Perak, *bendahara* (prime minister) and military commander. He expanded

Melaka's power along the west coast and to Singapore and the Bintan Islands.

By 1500, Melaka was the leading port in Southeast Asia, drawing Chinese, Indian, Javanese and Arab merchants. Governed with diplomacy by the great *bendahara* Tun Mutahir, the sultanate asserted its supremacy over virtually the whole Malay Peninsula and across the Strait of Malacca to the east coast of Sumatra. Prosperity was based entirely on the entrepôt trade: importing textiles from India, spices from Indonesia, silk and porcelain from China, gold and pepper from Sumatra, camphor from Borneo and sandalwood from Timor.

Portuguese conquest

In the 16th century, Melaka fell victim to Portugal's anti-Muslim crusade in the campaign to break the Arab-Venetian domination of commerce between Asia and Europe. The first visit of a Portuguese ship to Melaka in 1509 ended badly, as embittered Gujarati Indian merchants poisoned the atmosphere against the Portuguese. Two years later, the Portuguese sent their fleet, led by Afonso de Albuquerque, to seize Melaka. No match for the Portuguese invaders, the court fled south, establishing a new centre of Malay Muslim power in Johor. Albuquerque built a fort and church on the site of the sultan's palace. He ruled the non-Portuguese community with Malay *kapitan* headmen and the foreigners' *shahbandars* (harbour masters). Relations were better with the merchants from China and India than with the Muslims.

The 130 years of Portuguese control proved precarious. They faced repeated assault from Malay forces, and malaria was a constant scourge. Unable or unwilling to court the old vassal Malay states or the *Orang Laut* pirates to patrol the seas, the new rulers forfeited their predecessors' monopoly in the Strait of Malacca and, with it, command of the Moluccas spice trade.

A carved stone wall at A'Famosa fort

They made little effort, despite the Jesuit presence in Asia, to convert local inhabitants to Christianity or to expand their territory. The original colony of 600 men intermarried with local women to form a large Eurasian community.

The Dutch take over

Intent on capturing a piece of the Portuguese trade in pepper and other spices, the Java-based Dutch joined the Malays in 1633 to blockade Melaka. This ended in a seven-month siege with the Portuguese surrender in 1641.

Unlike the Portuguese, the Dutch decided to do business with the Malays of Johor, who controlled the southern half of the peninsula together with Singapore and the Riau islands. Without ever regaining the supremacy of the old Melaka sultanate, Johor had become the strongest regional power. Meanwhile, fresh blood came in with the migration into the southern interior of Minangkabau farmers from Sumatra, while tough Bugis warriors from the east Indonesian Celebes (Sulawesi) roved across the peninsula. The Minangkabau custom of electing their leaders provided the model for rulership elections in modern federal Malaysia. Their confederation of states became today's Negeri Sembilan (Nine States), with Seremban as its capital.

In the 18th century, with the Dutch concentrating again on Java and the Moluccas, the Bugis took advantage of the vacuum by raiding Perak and Kedah, imposing their chieftains in Selangor and becoming the power behind the Johor throne.

British rule

The British had shown little interest in Malaya. That changed in 1786, when the Sultan of Kedah granted Francis Light, a representative of the East India Company, rights to the island of Penang and the strip of mainland coast called Province Wellesley (now Seberang Perai) as a counterweight to the demands of the Siamese and Burmese. Unlike Portuguese and Dutch trading posts, Penang was declared a duty-free zone, attracting settlers and traders. By 1801, the population was over 10,000, concentrated in the island's capital, George Town.

In 1805, a dashing EIC administrator, Thomas Stamford Bingley Raffles, came to Penang at the age of 24. His knowledge of Malay customs and language, and humanitarian vision, made him vital in Britain's expanding role in Malay affairs. Raffles secured his place in history by negotiating, in 1819, the creation of the Singapore trading post with the Sultan of Johor. Singapore became capital of the Straits Settlements – as the EIC called its Malay holdings, incorporating Penang and Melaka – and was the linchpin of Britain's 150-year regional presence.

Buffalo horns

The name *Minangkabau* roughly means 'buffalo horns' and is reflected in the distinctive upward curving roofs in museums and government offices built in the Minangkabau style.

The Straits Settlements were formed after the Anglo-Dutch Treaty of London (1824). This colonial carve-up partitioned the Malay world through the Strait of Malacca. The peninsula and Sumatra, after centuries of common language, religion and traditions, were divided. The islands south of Singapore, including Java and Sumatra, went to the Dutch. Peninsular Malaysia and northwest Borneo remained under British control. From 1826, British law was technically in force, but in practice few British people lived in the Straits, and local affairs were run by merchant leaders serving as unofficial *kapitans*.

Apart from the few Malays in the settlements' rural communities of Province Wellesley and the Melaka hinterland, the majority still lived inland. Unity among them and the east coast communities trading with the Siamese, Indochinese and Chinese came from their shared rice economy, language, culture, and customs inherited from the Melaka sultanate.

Province Wellesley acted as a mainland buffer for Penang, and Melaka similarly turned its back on affairs in the hinterland. When Kedah and Perak sought British help against Siam, the British took the easier option of siding with the Siamese to quell revolts. But in the 1870s, under the Colonial Office, the profits gained from exporting Malayan tin through Singapore forced the British to take an active role in Malay affairs.

The lucrative tin mines of Kuala Lumpur, of Sungai Ujong (Negeri Sembilan), and of Larut and Taiping (Perak) were run for the Malay rulers by Chinese managers and labourers. Chinese secret societies waged gang wars for the control of the mines, bringing tin production to a halt at a time when world demand was at a peak. In 1874, Governor Andrew Clarke persuaded the Malay rulers of Perak and Selangor to accept British Residents as advisors; in return, Britain offered protection.

It began badly. Within a year the Resident in Perak, James Birch, was assassinated after efforts to impose direct British control. Subsequent British advisors served on a consultative

City Hall in George Town

state council alongside Malay ruler, chiefs and Chinese *kapitans*. Birch's successor in Perak, Hugh Low (1877–89), was more successful. Reforms he persuaded the ruler to accept included organising revenue collection, dismantling slavery and regulating land. Unity was enhanced by the growing network of railways and roads. Governor Frederick Weld (1880–87) extended the residency system to Negeri Sembilan and the more recalcitrant Pahang, where Sultan Wan Ahmad was forced to open the Kuantan tin mines to British prospectors.

A Federation of Malay States – Selangor, Perak, Negeri Sembilan and Pahang – was proclaimed in 1896 to coordinate economics and administration. Frank Swettenham became first Resident-General, with Kuala Lumpur as the capital.

The 'White Rajahs' of Borneo

In the 19th century, Borneo remained undeveloped. Balanini pirates, fervent Muslims, disputed the coast of northeastern

James Brooke, Rajah of Sarawak

Borneo (modern-day Sabah) with the sultanate of Brunei. Sarawak's coast and interior were controlled by the Iban, Sea Dayak pirates and Land Dayak slash-and-burn farmers. The region's only major resource was the gold and antimony mined by the Chinese in the Sarawak River valley.

In 1839, the Governor of Singapore sent James Brooke (1803–68) to promote trade with the Sultan of Brunei. In exchange for helping the regent end a revolt by Malay chiefs, Brooke was made Rajah of Sarawak in 1841, with his capital in Kuching. He tried to halt the Dayaks' piracy and head-hunting (believed to bring spiritual energy to their communities), while defending their more 'morally acceptable' customs. His attempts to limit the opium trade met with resistance from the Chinese in Bau, who revolted. His counterattack with Dayak warriors drove the Chinese out of Bau. Thereafter, Chinese settlement was discouraged.

In 1863, Brooke retired, handing Sarawak over to his nephew, Charles. A better administrator and financier, Charles Brooke imposed his efficient lifestyle. He brought Dayak leaders onto his ruling council but favoured the colonial practice of divide and rule by pitting one tribe against another.

In 1877, northeast Borneo (Sabah) was 'rented' from the Sultan of Brunei by British businessman Alfred Dent, who was operating a royal charter for the British North Borneo Company. This region was grouped together with Sarawak and Brunei in 1888 as a British protectorate, named North Borneo.

The early 20th century

The British extended their control over the peninsula by putting together the whole panoply of colonial administration. At the same time, the tin industry, which had been dominated by the Chinese, passed increasingly into the hands of Westerners, who employed modern technology. Petroleum had been found in northern Borneo, at Miri, and in Brunei, and the Anglo-Dutch Shell company used Singapore for exporting.

But the major breakthrough for the Malay economy was rubber, developed by the director of Singapore Botanical Gardens, Henry Ridley. World demand increased with the motor car and electrical industries, and rocketed during World War I. By 1920, Malaya was producing 53 percent of the world's rubber. Together with effective control of the rubber and tin industries, the British firmly controlled government.

The census of 1931 was an alarm signal for the Malay national consciousness. Bolstered by an influx of immigrants to meet the rubber and tin booms, non-Malays now slightly outnumbered the indigenous population. The Depression of 1929 stepped up ethnic competition in the shrinking job market, and nationalism developed to safeguard Malay interests against the Chinese and Indians rather than British imperialism.

Conservative Muslim intellectuals and community leaders came together at the Pan-Malayan Malay Congress in Kuala Lumpur in 1939. The following year, they were joined in Singapore by representatives from Sarawak and Brunei.

Japanese occupation

The Pacific War actually began on Malaysia's east coast. On 8 December 1941, an hour before Pearl Harbor was bombed,

Japanese troops landed on Sabak Beach (see page 75). Japan coveted Malaya's natural resources of rubber, tin and oil and the port of Singapore. The stated aim of the Japanese invasion was a 'Greater East Asia Co-Prosperity Sphere', appealing to Malay nationalism to throw off Western imperialism.

Not expecting a land attack, Commonwealth troops on the peninsula were ill-prepared. The landings were launched from bases ceded to the Japanese by Marshal Pétain's French colonial officials in Indochina and were backed by fighter jets.

Japanese infantry poured in from Thailand to capture airports in Kedah and Kelantan. Kuala Lumpur fell on 11 January 1942 and, five weeks later, Singapore was captured.

If Japanese treatment of Allied prisoners of war in Malaya was notoriously brutal, the attitude towards Asian civilians was more ambivalent. At first, the Japanese curtailed the privileges of the Malay rulers and forced them to pay homage to the Japanese Emperor. Then, to gain Malay support, the Japanese upheld their prestige, restored pensions and preserved their authority, at least in Malay customs and Islamic religion.

The Chinese were massacred. From 1943 Chinese communists led the resistance in the Malayan People's Anti-Japanese Army, aided by the British, to prepare for an Allied return.

The 'Emergency'

The Japanese surrender left in place a 7,000-strong resistance army led by Chinese communists. Before disbanding, the army wrought revenge on Malays who had collaborated with the Japanese. This in turn sparked a brief wave of racial violence between Malays and Chinese.

To match their long-term stake in the country's prosperity, the Chinese and Indians wanted political equality with the Malays. Nationalists in the new United Malays National Organisation (UMNO) resented this 'foreign' intrusion imposed by 19th-century economic development. To give the

Malays safeguards against economically dominant Chinese and Indians, the British created the new Federation of Malaya in 1948. Strong government under a High Commissioner left powers in the hands of the states' Malay rulers. Crown colony status was granted to Northern Borneo and Singapore, the latter excluded from the Federation because of its Chinese majority. The Chinese, considering their loyalty to the Allied cause in World War II, felt betrayed. Some turned to the Chinese-led Malayan Communist Party (MCP).

The National Monument in KL

Four months after the creation of the Federation, three European rubber planters were murdered in Perak – the first victims in a guerrilla war launched by communist rebels. The British sent in troops, but the killing continued. The violence reached a climax in 1951, with the assassination of High Commissioner Henry Gurney.

Gurney's successor, General Gerald Templer, stepped in to deal with the 'Emergency'. He intensified military action, while cutting the political grass from under the communists' feet. Templer stepped up self-government, increased Chinese access to full citizenship and admitted those of Chinese origin for the first time to the Malayan Civil Service.

Under Cambridge-trained lawyer Tunku Abdul Rahman, brother of the Sultan of Kedah, UMNO's conservative

Malays formed an alliance with the English-educated bourgeoisie of the Malayan Chinese and Malayan Indian Congress. During the Emergency, Chinese and Indian community leaders sought a solution. The Alliance won 51 of 52 seats in the 1955 election by promising a fair, multiracial constitution.

Independence

Independence or *merdeka* (freedom) came in 1957, and the Emergency ended three years later. The Alliance's English-educated elite imagined that multiracial integration would come about through education and employment. With a bicameral government under a constitutional monarchy, the Federation made Malay the compulsory language and Islam the official religion. Primary education could be in Chinese, Indian or English, but secondary education was in Malay.

The Prime Minister's palatial residence in Putrajaya

Tunku Abdul Rahman, the first prime minister, reversed his party's anti-Chinese policy by offering Singapore a place in the Federation. With the defeat of Singapore's moderate Progressive Party by left-wing radicals, Tunku Abdul Rahman feared the creation of a communist state on his doorstep. As a counterweight to the Singapore Chinese, he brought in the North Borneo states of Sabah and Sarawak, granting them special privileges for their indigenous populations and funds to help to develop their economies.

To embrace the enlarged territory, the Federation took on the new name of Malaysia in September 1963, but Singapore, with its multiracial policies, sought to dismantle Malay privileges. Singapore's effort to reorganise political parties on a social and economic, rather than ethnic, basis misread Malay feelings. Riots broke out in 1964, and Tunku Abdul Rahman was forced to expel Singapore from the Federation in 1965.

Four days of racial riots in the federal capital in 1969 led to the suspension of the constitution and a state of emergency. The constitution was not restored until February 1971. The riots were a warning for the government, which was passing controversial legislation, such as the granting of special rights to Malays and the restriction of public gatherings.

Tun Abdul Razak became prime minister after the retirement of Tunku Abdul Rahman in 1970. Under his administration, emphasis was placed on improving the status of Malays and 'other indigenous peoples'. The government's aim was to broaden the distribution of wealth held by Malays.

On Abdul Razak's death in 1976, Datuk Hussein Onn, a son of the founder of the UMNO, became prime minister, and UMNO became stronger just as Malaysian exports were growing. Combined political and economic strength set a sound base for Datuk Seri Dr Mahathir Mohamad when he became prime minister in July 1981.

Under Dr Mahathir, Malaysia achieved remarkable economic prosperity. Rubber and tin declined in importance, but were supplemented by palm oil plantations, discoveries of petroleum and natural gas reserves off Borneo's north coast and the peninsula's east coast, and developments in manufacturing and tourism. Timber, which during the 1970s and 1980s brought valuable revenue, was reduced to conserve forests. In recent years, manufacturing, particularly electronics, represented a new direction away from a dependence on commodity exports.

The 21st century

Malaysia entered the new millennium as a wealthy country with a sound economy. In October 2003, Datuk Seri Abdullah Ahmad Badawi took over the premiership, following Dr Mahathir's retirement. In the 2008 election, the coalition government received its biggest backlash in 50 years with the opposition winning the states of Kelantan, Selangor, Kedah, Penang and Perak. Voters expressed their concern over Badawi's leadership and his government's lack of direction. In 2009, Najib Abdul Razak took over as Malaysia's sixth prime minister, and started repairing the damage by introducing a multi-million-Ringgit campaign called '1 Malaysia' to convince Malaysians that unity is a priority of the government. In practice, however, the government continues to woo non-Malay voters and the Malay electorate with different promises.

Mounted police in Melaka

Historical Landmarks

c.1.8 million BC Discovery of a stone hand-axe indicates habitation in Lenggong Valley, Perak.

c.235,000 BC Earliest known habitation in Borneo at Mansuli Valley.

c.10,000–2,500 BC Austronesians, the ancestors of Borneon natives and Malays, settle in the region.

AD200–700 Buddhist-Hindu trading kingdoms in Kedah and Sarawak.

c.1400 Founding of Melaka by Srivijaya prince Parameswara.

1411 Parameswara converts to Islam, establishes sultanate of Melaka.

c.1459–77 Melaka's empire expands.

1511 Melaka falls to the Portuguese.

1641 Dutch take over Melaka from the Portuguese.

1786 The British occupy Penang.

1826 Penang, Melaka and Singapore made Straits Settlements under the British.

1841 James Brooke established as Rajah of Sarawak.

1941–5 Japanese occupation.

1945 British reoccupy Malaya.

1948–60 Communist insurgency – the 'Emergency'.

1955 First general elections in the peninsula; victory for Alliance coalition.

1957 Malaya becomes independent, with Tunku Abdul Rahman as PM.

1963 Malaysia is formed, comprising Malaya, Singapore, Sabah and Sarawak.

1965 Singapore leaves Malaysia.

1969 Four days of racial riots, known as the 'May 13 incident', lead to a state of emergency.

1981–2003 Dr Mahathir Mohamad is the country's longest-serving PM.

1998 Kuala Lumpur hosts the Commonwealth Games.

2003 Abdullah Ahmad Badawi becomes PM, then wins the 2004 election.

2008 Government wins election but with reduced majority as the opposition takes five states.

2009 Mohd Najib Tun Abdul Razak takes over as the sixth PM.

2012 A rally demanding electoral reform ends with police firing tear gas and water cannons.

WHERE TO GO

Setting your priorities in Malaysia before you set off is essential to making your trip both pleasant and satisfying. Happily, many destinations offer a key that active travellers will be searching for, such as exploring Malaysia's culture and history or engaging in a sport like scuba diving. Often there is an added bonus: a nearby forest or a beachside resort.

Malaysia's well-developed transport infrastructure – rail, road and air – also offers the chance to step away from rigid planning if you desire to stay an extra day by the beach or want to do some more extensive shopping. Caution is needed if you are not used to a hot and humid climate and you may have to do a little extra planning when heading out on tour, trekking or just lazing by the pool.

Planning the journey

The towns hold a mirror to Malaysia's ethnic blend of Malay, Chinese, Indians and Eurasians, living side by side or in their separate neighbourhoods. The northeast coast of Malaysia, especially between Kota Bharu and Kuantan, is one of the best places to see traditional Malay life with its rich Muslim culture, particularly evident in the *kampungs* (villages) of the interior. Step back into Malaysia's history in the port towns of Melaka (also known as Malacca) or George Town, where colonial rivals once battled for supremacy. Your attention will also be captured by the beauty of the many mosques, temples, churches and shrines as the country's faithful practise their beliefs. In Melaka, observe the way of life of the Nyonyas and Babas, the oldest locally born Chinese community, and its more modern manifestation in Penang.

Sunset at Batu Feringghi beach

Bukit Bintang in the KLCC

Beyond urban limits you will find many opportunities to enjoy rural and forested Malaysia. But finding your way around the various rainforests, coral reefs or marine reserves can be bewildering if you plunge in unprepared. Unless you already have some experience in the region, use the services of one of the many first-class local tour operators (see page 169).

Malaysia has done a fine job of providing visitors with access to its natural assets without 'taming' these resources too much. At the heart of the peninsula, the huge Taman Negara gives you the most comprehensive view of rainforest animals and plants in their natural state. A more 'compact' approach is possible on the islands, such as Tioman or Langkawi.

On the island of Borneo, the great natural attractions are Sarawak's caves at Niah and Mulu, river cruises with a visit to tribal longhouses, Sabah's national parks of Gunung Kinabalu and the offshore islands, and the Sepilok Orang-utan Sanctuary. If your main desire is to escape the coastal heat, highland retreats will refresh and invigorate, by offering a chance to enjoy what was once the exclusive domain of colonial administrators.

White sandy beaches and gentle sea breezes are for many the perfect recipe for a holiday from the stresses of modern life, and in Malaysia the offerings are plentiful. Whether on the peninsula or in the marine parks of Sabah and Sarawak, you'll find many opportunities to bask and laze under the tropical sun (remember to use sunscreen and drink plenty of water to avoid sunburn and dehydration).

On the west coast the best beaches are on the island resorts of Pangkor and Langkawi. Unspoiled stretches of sand can also be found on the east coast, from Pantai Cahaya Bulan, north of Kota Bharu, down to Beserah, north of Kuantan. Further south are the resorts of Tioman Island and Desaru. In East Malaysia, Kuching and Kota Kinabalu have fine resort hotels.

THE CENTRE

Malaysia's prosperity in recent decades is most evident in the central region of the peninsula, where signs of wealth abound, from the international airport to KL's dramatic skyline, to members of the middle class driving Malaysian-made Proton sedans on six-lane highways. But even as new light-rail systems wind through KL, progress has not entirely buried the past under chrome and concrete. Still thriving are the old commercial areas that brought so much wealth to the city and country.

Kuala Lumpur

At times **Kuala Lumpur** ❶ appears to be a maze of pedestrian-unfriendly overpasses and expressways. But the city opens to islands of almost forest-like tree-cover before descending again into lively markets surrounded by the buildings that rise above the city's busy streets. Visitors may initially be drawn to the 88-storey Petronas Twin Towers or Menara Kuala Lumpur (Kuala Lumpur Tower), which are symbols of modern KL. But the more fascinating splendours of the past are at street level, where distinctive neo-Gothic styles are beautifully preserved. Chinatown itself remains a hive of activity, located not far from pungent spice shops and ornate Hindu temples.

The Historic Centre

KL's main historic quarter lies near Jalan Sultan Hishamuddin, where, on the east side of the broad avenue, is the **Sultan Abdul Samad Building**. The crypto-Moorish Federal Secretariat, once the Supreme Court and High Court but now housing government offices, was begun in 1894 (finished in 1897) and capped with three copper onion-shaped domes. One tops a clock tower 40m (120ft) high that bears a similarity to London's Big Ben.

Playing football in the shadow of the KLCC skyline

On the western side of the boulevard is the **Dataran Merdeka** (Independence Square) **Ⓐ**: it was here that members of the mock-Tudor **Royal Selangor Club** (1884) took time off from the affairs of the Empire to play cricket. On the wide lawn, cheers greeted independence on 31 August 1957. **St Mary's Anglican Cathedral** is on the square's northern side. The oldest church in KL, it began life in 1887 as a wooden shack on Bukit Aman before being relocated here.

The Sultan Abdul Samad Building

Walk southwards to the bridge at Leboh Pasar Besar to view **Masjid Jamek**. Since 1909 this building has marked the confluence of the Sungai Gombak and Sungai Klang, where the city's roots were set down. It was here also that tin miners loaded supplies to be sent upriver and unloaded their tin for shipment west to Port Klang. It was designed in 1907 by British architect A.B. Hubbock in an Indian Moghul style: three-pointed domes over the prayer hall, two minarets and balustrades above an arcade of cusped arches – the whole predominantly gleaming white, with pink terracotta brick. Turn around to see one of the most striking skyscrapers – the 35-storey **Dayabumi Complex** (1970) that integrates traditional Islamic architectural themes – pointed arches, delicate open tracery – with otherwise modern design. Behind it is the **Pejabat Pos Besar** (General Post Office).

Hubbock also designed the **Malaysian Railway** buildings, located south on Jalan Sultan Hishamuddin. The old station

A minaret atop the Old Kuala Lumpur Railway Station

(completed in 1911 and renovated in 1986) resembles a sultan's palace and is more attractive than the sombre brown headquarters building opposite. A fine example of Moorish architecture, it reflects the Ottoman and Moghul glory of the 13th and 14th centuries. While it is still a stop on the suburban network, the city's main rail hub is now KL Sentral, situated southwest of here near **Muzium Negara** (National Museum) on Jalan Damansara. Opened in 1963, the museum blends modern and traditional Malay design. Five main galleries cover such subjects as history, national sports and natural history.

Near the Old Railway Station

Across from the Old Kuala Lumpur Railway Station is **Masjid Negara** (National Mosque), a modern complex covering over 5 hectares (13 acres). On Friday and other important religious days it can house 8,000 worshippers under the tent-like stone roof of its Grand Hall. Above it all is a minaret 73m (239ft) high, with a balcony from which the muezzin calls to prayer. Opposite Masjid Negara's car park is the splendid **Islamic Arts Museum Malaysia B** on Jalan Lembah Perdana, which showcases the art and culture of the Islamic world.

Taman Botani Perdana (Perdana Botanical Gardens)

West of Masjid Negara are the **Perdana Botanical Gardens** (formerly the Lake Gardens), 101 hectares (250 acres) of parkland landscaped in 1888 while Frank Swettenham was British Resident. A popular place for picnicking, jogging and resting beneath the trees, it features a boating lake, a butterfly farm, orchid garden, bird park and the **National Planetarium**.

On a hill at the northern end of the park across Jalan Parlimen, the **Tugu Peringatan Negara** (National Monument) commemorates Malaysia's unsettled history through the Emergency (see page 26). The bronze sculpture was designed by Felix de Weldon. Also on the monument grounds is a **Cenotaph** to the British Commonwealth's dead of the two World Wars. West of the monument, outside the park, is **Parliament House**, which holds the sessions of the Senate and House of Representatives and is not open to the public.

Across the river going east from the Dayabumi Complex is the old **Pasar Seni** (Central Market), set in an attractive art deco building (1936) in pastel blue and pink with a bold, bright skylit roof. Clothes and arts and crafts have replaced the fish, meat and vegetables that used to be sold here.

Chowing down at a hawker stall on Jalan Petaling

Chinatown

Southeast from the Central Market lie the exotic offerings of Chinatown at **Jalan Petaling** Ⓖ and the surrounding streets. Here you will discover an enclave of pre-war Chinese shophouses sheltering, among other businesses, Chinese apothecaries who display their medicines in porcelain jars, a multitude of restaurants and stalls, fortune-tellers and pet shops. At night, when Jalan Petaling is closed to traffic, the area really comes alive. Pedlars sell replica watches, CDs and DVDs, clothing, jewellery and ornaments; the side streets are full of open-air restaurants offering barbecued meats, seafood, noodles, rice-pots and do-it-yourself 'steam-boats' (see page 150).

Past the Jalan Tun H.S. Lee and Jalan Tun Tan Cheng Lock junction is the **Sin Sze Si Ya Temple**, founded by Yap Ah Loy, once the *kapitan* (headman) of KL's early community. The largest temple is **Chan See Shu Yuen Association** on Jalan Petaling, built in 1906 and dedicated to Chong Wah, a Sung Dynasty emperor. It also marks Chinatown's southern boundary.

An arresting display of colour comes in the form of the **Sri Maha Mariamman Hindu Temple** on Jalan Tun H.S. Lee. It was built in the style of a south Indian *gopuram* (temple gate-house-tower), covered with a riot of colourful statuary from the Hindu pantheon. First erected in 1873, it was shunted across to its present site to make way for the railway station in 1855, and it is from here the annual Thaipusam pilgrimage to Batu Caves (see page 45) commences.

Southwest of Chinatown is Jalan Tun Sambanthan, which leads past KL Sentral and through the heart of **Little India** in **Brickfields ⓓ**, where you will find restaurants serving vegetarian fare, delectable curries, sinfully sweet candies and grocery shops alongside numerous boutiques selling Indian saris and Punjabi suits, flower stalls and pet shops.

Northeast of the historic centre

KL's 'Golden Triangle' is a modern office, entertainment and shopping district. Within this triangle, at the edge of the **Bukit Nanas Forest Recreational Park,** is the **Menara Kuala Lumpur** (Kuala Lumpur Tower) ⓔ on Jalan Punchak, which opened in 1996 and rises to 421m (1,381ft). The non-stop lift takes 55 seconds from ground to the observatory, and offers the city's best views.

Nearby is the city's tallest landmark. The **Petronas Twin Towers**  are located north of the triangle and part of the **Kuala Lumpur City Centre (KLCC)**. The sky bridge on the 41st floor and the observation deck on the 86th floor are open to the public. Below there is a concert hall, upmarket shopping mall and the interactive science centre Petrosains.

Skirting north of the 'Golden Triangle' and going past the twin towers is the Jalan Ampang, 9km (5.5 miles) long, where you can see the **tin magnates' man-**

Old and new architecture visibly contrasts in KL

sions that remain standing. One of the best preserved is the Dewan Tunku Abdul Rahman, built in 1935 by Chinese tin and rubber mogul Eu Tong Sen, which is near the Jalan Sultan Ismail junction. Nowadays it is the **Malaysia Tourism Centre (MaTiC)**, which provides travel advice, brochures, Internet access, banking and a 24-hour tourist-police counter.

Markets

Day and night markets remain popular with Malaysians for cheap products and excellent local food. They are ideal for soaking up local colour and atmosphere. One of the cheapest daytime markets is at Chow Kit at the corner of Jalan

Raja Alang and Jalan Haji Hussein. Southeast of Chow Kit is Kampung Baru, a night market catering to more traditional tastes. This **Pasar Minggu** (Sunday Market) begins on Saturday evening and trades on into the early hours of Sunday morning.

Selangor

Around Kuala Lumpur is the state of **Selangor**, an area that grew rich on tin and today is Malaysia's wealthiest and most developed state. While the emphasis in this region is clearly on industry, information technology and administration, there are a number of sites well worth visiting.

Petaling Jaya and Sunway City

On the campus of the University of Malaysia is the **Museum of Asian Art**, with exhibits of regional pottery and ceramics dating from as early as the 9th century. Within the same campus, the **Rimba Ilmu** (Forest of Knowledge) is a tropical botanical garden but in a rainforest setting; it showcases over 1,600 species of the country's flora, as well as those from Indonesia. **Sunway Lagoon,** near suburban Subang Jaya, is known for its rides and water attractions, including a beach with artificial waves for surfing. It's great fun for the family.

Jalan Alor is lively at night with hawker stalls

Batu Caves

The giant **Batu Caves** ❷ are a popular excursion 45 minutes' drive north of KL, just off the Ipoh Road. Set in limestone cliffs hidden in the forest, they were 'discovered' in 1878 by a group of explorers. The caves were a hideout for anti-Japanese communist guerrillas during World War II. Now transformed into a Hindu shrine, they receive the most attention during the Thaipusam Festival celebrated in the early months of each year.

There are in fact dozens of impressive limestone caves attracting botanists and zoologists to study their unique flora and fauna, but only three are accessible to the general public. At the top of a 272-step staircase is the **Temple Cave**, the most breathtaking of the three, with its architectural columns of lofty stalactites and stalagmites. At the foot of the

At the Sunway Lagoon Theme Park

hill, a bridge over a Koi pond leads to the **Cave Villa**, with three indoor galleries – the Valluvar Kottam, where verses of the ancient Tamil poet Thiruvalluvar are painted directly on stone tablets; a reptile gallery; and the art gallery, which displays colourful statues of Hindu deities. There is also a 15-minute cultural dance performance every hour. After exiting the Temple Cave, about a third of the way down the main steps, turn right for a guided tour of the **Dark Cave's** ecosystem and geological formations. Prior booking is necessary if you wish to explore further and crawl through limestone passages.

The FRIM Canopy Walkway

Templer Park

Further north (another 9km/6 miles along the Ipoh Road)
from the Batu Caves is **Templer Park**, which offers an insight
into a Malaysian rainforest for those with little time to venture
into the major national parks. Named after Britain's last High
Commissioner, Sir Gerald Templer, and covering an area of
1,200 hectares (2,965 acres), the rainforest comes complete
with waterfalls, rushing streams and caves to explore in the
Bukit Takun limestone cliffs. There are several forest trails,
with the highest point being **Bukit Takun,** 740m (2,428ft),
on the western side of the river in the park's northern corner.

FRIM

For a rainforest experience with lofty views of the forest, head
west of Batu Caves to the 600ha (1,480-acre) **Forest Research
Institute of Malaysia**. Purchase your **Canopy Walkway**
ticket from the visitor's information centre before you head

up the trail that leads to the Canopy Walkway, 30m (100ft) high, which has good views of the forest canopy.

Kuala Selangor
Northwest of Shah Alam is Kuala Selangor, on the Sungai Selangor estuary, where you can see large flocks of migratory birds (Sept–Oct) at the **Kuala Selangor Nature Park**. After dinner in one of the seafood restaurants at **Pasir Penambang**, head upriver to **Kampung Kuantan** for a boat ride to see the synchronous flashing of fireflies; it is best to appreciate this natural wonder on a new moon night.

Putrajaya
Located 25km (15.5 miles) south of KL is the federal administrative capital of **Putrajaya,** with its stately government buildings, mosques and public gardens. If dressed appropriately, there is the Persian-inspired **Masjid Putra** to visit during non-prayer time. Or walk down to the lakeside, and at the end

Thaipusam Festival in the Batu Caves

The Batu Caves are the focus of the great Thaipusam Festival celebrating Lord Murugan receiving a sacred spear with which to vanquish the sources of evil.

Every January or February (depending on the moon) thousands of Hindus gather to do penitence for past sins. The most fervent of them punish themselves by having their tongues or cheeks pierced with skewers, and hooks inserted in their bodies. Some also carry a *kavadi* (a frame bearing peacock feathers and statuettes of deities). Some simply carry jars of milk, rose water, coconut or sugar-cane juice. During Thaipusam, as many as 500,000 people will crowd around the Batu Caves.

For tourists, the climb in humid heat up 272 steps to the cave-shrine entrance may be penitence enough.

of the Souq Putrajaya bazaar is the jetty for the **Cruise Tasik Putrajaya**; sunset is the best time to tour the lake.

Day trips from Kuala Lumpur

Beyond KL, the British colonial past – whose structures now more often stand in the shadow of KL's skyscrapers – continues to echo through hill stations. These have now become resorts, set among golf courses, gardens and orchards in the mountain ranges of the peninsula's interior. Retreats within easier reach of KL – Fraser's Hill and Genting Highlands – draw families for holidays.

Genting Highlands

Nearest of the highland resort areas to Kuala Lumpur, 51km (32 miles) away, is **Genting Highlands,** which rises to 2,000m (6,560ft). Descriptions of the resort and hotel complex vary from 'big and bold' to a 'one-stop destination for fantasy, excitement and adventure.' You'll find a wide range of facilities, including theme parks with cinemas, boat rides, restaurants and ten-pin bowling. The resort's casino is Malaysia's only such legal gambling house. Further down the hill, and less misty and wet, is the 18-hole golf course at the **Awana Golf and Country Club**.

Fraser's Hill

In contrast to Genting Highlands, this charming, old-fashioned hill station, 100km (60 miles) northwest of KL, is built across seven hills, its highest point being 1,500m (4,920ft) in the Titiwangsa Range. These days, **Fraser's Hill** offers a cool and peaceful retreat. The resort was named after Louis James Fraser, an English adventurer and scoundrel, who dealt in mule hides, tin, opium and gambling. Fraser had disappeared mysteriously before the hill station came into being in 1910.

Overlooking the Genting Highlands

En route to the **Gap** gate at the foothill of Fraser's Hill, a signpost that reads 'Emergency Historical Site' marks where British High Commissioner Sir Henry Gurney was killed during the communist insurgency in 1951. The narrow road between the Gap and Fraser's Hill is an alternating, one-way traffic system unless the secondary road (which is more prone to landslides), about 1km (0.6 miles) after the Gap gate, is open for exiting traffic. There is a wide range of accommodation, from stone bungalows to hotels and resorts, as well as a nine-hole golf course, playgrounds, archery and horse riding to enjoy.

Several nature trails are marked out through the nearby forests, and the wealth of birdlife means that forest walks are particularly enjoyable. Birdwatchers should look out for more than 270 species of birds, which may be seen in the immediate area. Montane species like the stunning Cutia, although a Himalayan bird, are found here. Eagles are easy to spot soaring above the trees.

THE NORTHWEST

In the far north, Penang is both a holiday destination and a commercial centre, while closer to the border with Thailand, Langkawi Island is Southeast Asia's first Geopark and a leading resort for those in search of white sands, gentle seas, a scenic landscape and duty-free goods. While Ipoh is Perak's state capital, made rich on tin, and Kuala Kangsar is the leisurely, royal state capital, the former mining towns of Papan and Gopeng are steeped in history. From Simpang Pulai in Perak, it is easy to access the cool breezes of Cameron Highlands, where the English palate for tea (on a plantation scale) and strawberries thrives in the adjacent state of Pahang. Other natural attractions – wild elephants in the interior forests at Belum-Temengor, birdwatching along the Perak coastline and beautiful beaches of Pulau Pangkor – make pleasant experiences.

Perak

A journey to Perak takes travellers into what was once the key region for Malaysia's economic prosperity. Tin, the basis for the state's wealth, was taken from diggings that claimed to be the largest such mines in the world. The wealth from the mines paid for many of the historical structures evident throughout the state. Perak, which means silver in Malay, is Peninsular Malaysia's second-largest state, reaching from Tanjung Malim in the south to the Thai border, covering some 21,000 sq km (8,108 sq miles). Its sultan's family is also the last to be able to trace its ancestry to the 16th-century sultans of Melaka.

The journey north from KL either by train or car takes you through a captivating landscape of forests and plantations, reaching back from the coastal plains to climb the blue hills of the Titiwangsa Range.

A Chinese coffee shop in Ipoh

Ipoh

Once the harbour for all incoming junks and sampans from the Strait of Malacca (Selat Melaka) through the Perak River, the city of **Ipoh** is on the Kinta River 220km (135 miles) north of KL. Ipoh offers good accommodation and amenities, including a range of restaurants with Chinese specialities, such as steamed chicken with bean sprouts and noodles.

Colonial influences are clearly evident in the **railway station**, whose Moghul architecture is reminiscent of KL's old station and is locally nicknamed 'the Taj Mahal'. The **High Court** and **Hong Kong and Shanghai Banking Corporation (HSBC)** buildings are also excellent examples of architecture from the Edwardian era. Other memories of the British presence are in the **clock tower**, commemorating the first British resident of Perak, James Birch, who was assassinated in 1875. **St Michael's School** and the **Royal Ipoh Club** are also monuments of the colonial era.

Picking tea at the Sungai Palas Estate in the
Cameron Highlands

Around Jalan Dato' Sagor and the nearby streets are some
of the best-preserved examples of **Chinese architecture**
in Malaysia. For an insight into the local tin-mining industry, visit the excellent **Muzium Geologi** on Jalan Sultan
Azlan Shah. In addition to exhibits of Perak's rich variety
of minerals, ores and fossils, there are models of tin-mining
equipment.

Outside the city, amid vast caves in limestone outcrops, are a
number of Buddhist temples. In the south the **Sam Poh Tong
Temple,** founded in 1912, is located within high limestone
caves and cavities near Gunung Rapat and is home to a group
of monks and nuns. Six kilometres (4 miles) north of Ipoh
is the **Perak Tong**, built in 1926 by a Buddhist priest from
China. Here the main attraction is a 13m (41ft) sitting Buddha
within the darkened cavern; altogether there are more than 40
Buddha statues.

Day Trips from Ipoh

Around Ipoh there are plenty of historical and natural sights to see and experience – from prehistoric art to historical buildings, show caves and tropical rainforests to a night safari and gorgeous beaches. Simpang Pulai also offers easy access to highland tea plantations in the neighbouring state of Pahang.

Spotting a tapir

The tapir is remarkable for two features: its short, overlapping snout that resembles the sawed-off trunk of an elephant, and its unique body colouring – black at the front, white in the middle and back, with black rear legs. With luck you may spot one in Tanah Rata.

Tambun

About 15 minutes' drive east of Ipoh is **Tambun**, which has the peninsula's largest rock art site at Gua Tambun, a cliff face with over 600 Neolithic-period rock paintings depicting human and animal motifs. Nearby is the Lost World of Tambun, a popular water theme park with rides, a hot spring and spa.

Cameron Highlands

Heading south from Ipoh on the North-South Expressway, exit at the Simpang Pulai interchange, turn right and follow signs to **Cameron Highlands ❸** in the state of Pahang. The finest of the British-inspired hill stations, 85km (53 miles) from Ipoh, stands on a splendid plateau in rolling green valleys, surrounded by the rugged peaks of the Titiwangsa Range, the tallest of which is Gunung Brinchang, at 2,031m (6,664ft). Located over 1,520m (4,987ft) above sea level, Cameron Highlands offers great relief amid morning mists and cool breezes. The hill station was named after William Cameron, a British surveyor who in 1885 reported the finding of the 'fine plateau'. The Highlands still hide the answer to the mysterious

Orang Asli house in the Cameron Highlands

disappearance of wealthy American Thai-silk entrepreneur Jim Thompson, who went missing one evening in 1967 after setting off for a stroll while on holiday at the hill station.

Spread over three districts are the townships of **Brinchang**, **Tanah Rata** (the main township) and **Ringlet**. Brinchang is known for its vegetable farms, flower nurseries, fruit gardens and tea plantations. Tanah Rata has hotels, good Chinese and Indian restaurants, and English-style tearooms serving the local Cameronian brew together with cakes and locally grown strawberries with cream. The main tea plantations are **Cameron Bharat Plantation** and Boh's **Sungei Palas Tea Estate**. The latter features a **Tea Centre** (Tue–Sun), where you can learn about tea manufacturing, and sample various blends while enjoying great views of the estate.

Accommodation options in Tanah Rata vary depending on your budget, from international-class resorts to moderately priced guesthouses.

The cooler climate makes forest walks here a special pleasure. Two relatively well-marked paths from Tanah Rata, which are easy enough for the whole family, lead to swimming and picnic spots at **Parit Falls** and **Robinson Falls**. Other more challenging choices, for which you should enlist the help of a guide, take you up to **Gunung Jasar**

Forest exploration

The forests, especially those in the Cameron Highlands, were once strongholds for the rebels during the Communist Emergency. Some caution is required when venturing into them as many paths have few or no signposts; good maps are a must, and a guide is recommended for most trails.

(1,696m/5,564ft) and **Gunung Beremban** (1,841m/6,040ft). The best buys in Cameron are fresh flowers, fruit and vegetables. Continue 13km (7 miles) from Tanah Rata to reach Ringlet town, which offers very little that is special, apart from flower nurseries and access to some tea plantations.

For those using public transport, the Highlands can be reached by train on the KL–Butterworth line to Tapah Road Station and then to the hills by taxi. The scenery changes from bamboo and palms to a denser rainforest of lush greenery, and then, as the temperature drops and the more comfortable mountain air takes over, the montane oaks and laurels that are common in temperate climates. The old road, though shorter, is more circuitous than the new road from Simpang Pulai.

Papan

Half an hour south of Ipoh on Route 5, and then a right onto Route A188, is the ghost-like town of **Papan ❹**. Visit the home and dispensary of a World War II heroine, which is today a **Memorial to Sybil Kathigasu** (by prior appointment; mobile tel: 017-506 1875). Eurasian nurse Sybil Daly (later decorated with a George Medal for gallantry) and her medical doctor husband Dr A.C. Kathigasu supported the

Kuala Kangsar's Istana Kenangan

Malayan People's Anti-Japanese Army guerrillas by secretly providing them with medical care, medicines and information during the Japanese Occupation. They were, however, betrayed, caught and tortured by the Japanese. A one-hour tour of the **historical town** or nearby **Batu Gajah** town is also available, starting from the memorial.

Gopeng and surroundings

Further south and 25km (16 miles) from Ipoh is Gopeng, where the **Muzium Gopeng** displays antiques and tin-mining artefacts from the glorious past. Nearby is **Kampung Ulu Geroh,** whose indigenous people, the Orang Asli, can show you the beautiful **Rajah Brooke's Birdwing** (butterfly) and, if in bloom, the **Rafflesia**, the world's largest individual flower. Further southwards is the show cave of **Gua Tempurung,** the longest cave system in the peninsula, stretching more than 4.5km (3 miles).

Saved from the overgrowth of foliage in the past two decades, **Kellie's Castle** is a mansion 14km (9 miles) northwest of Gopengis. Construction was halted when its owner, rubber planter William Kellie Smith, died in Portugal in the mid-1920s.

Kuala Kangsar

Home to the sultans of Perak since the 15th century, **Kuala Kangsar** is built on a reach of the Perak River (Sungai Perak) 50km (32 miles) from Ipoh, just off the highway. The town has two royal palaces: the brash stone residence **Istana Iskandariah** and the more elegant traditional timbered **Istana Kenangan**, now used as a Royal Museum. The most striking building, set on a grass mound, is the **Masjid Ubudiah**, with its dome of glowing copper.

Belum-Temengor Forest Complex

About 144km (89 miles) northwest from Kuala Kangsar, the lush **Belum-Temengor Forest Complex** surrounds Perak's largest dam, offering visitors a chance to explore the rainforest with Orang Asli guides. The forest supports a wide range of animal and plant life, much of it endangered because of logging in the area. See all of the country's 10 hornbill species here, keep watch for wild elephants foraging for food in the evenings and, if in luck, catch sight of the rare Rafflesia flower.

Taiping

A 30-minute drive from Kuala Kangsar, the old mining town of **Taiping** , which means 'everlasting peace', is the former capital of Perak state. It has a magnificent 90-hectare (222-acre) park, **Lake Gardens**, landscaped from a tin mine abandoned in 1890. The grounds are now home to a Japanese garden and the **Taiping Zoo & Night Safari.**

Built in 1883, the **Perak Museum** houses an interesting display of ancient weapons and Orang Asli implements and is the

Pangkor Laut

oldest museum in Malaysia. On the way, you will pass **Taiping Prison**, used by the Japanese in World War II and then for guerrilla troops captured during the Emergency.

Beyond the Lake Gardens, the **Taiping War Cemetery** bears impressive witness to the peninsula's early role in the Pacific War against the Japanese. The tombs of soldiers of the Royal Australian Air Force, Indian Army Corps of Clerks, Ambulance Sepoy of the Indian Army Medical Corps and Royal Air Force reveal that many of them died on the very first day of active duty: 8 December 1941.

Once a tea estate, cool, cloud-enshrouded **Bukit Larut** (Maxwell Hill), 12km (7.5 miles) northeast of Taiping, is Malaysia's smallest and oldest hill station. At 1,035m (3,400ft) above sea level, it has great views when the misty rain-clouds break. Near the jeep terminal, several bungalows and rest houses offer rooms for rent, but you must book in advance.

Perak's coastline
About half an hour's drive from Taiping is the **Matang Mangrove Forest Reserve,** where you can visit traditional charcoal kilns and fishing villages or head towards **Kuala Gula Bird Sanctuary** to watch migratory birds en route to Australia (Aug–Dec).

Pulau Pangkor

The largest of the nine islands lying offshore in the Strait of Malacca is **Pulau Pangkor**. Its beaches offer aquatic activities and there are nearby forest walks. The ferry from Lumut, about 50km (31 miles) south of Taiping, to Pangkor Island takes 30–45 minutes. Berjaya Air also flies in from Sultan Abdul Aziz Shah Airport, near KL, daily except Tuesday and Thursday. Once there, you'll find the wide sands of the **Pantai Puteri Dewi** (Beach of the Beautiful Princess) along the 122-hectare (301-acre) island's northern shore. An adjoining private island and one of the most exclusive destinations in Asia, **Pangkor Laut** attracts well-heeled tourists.

Penang

On the northeast coast of **Pulau Pinang ❺** (meaning Betel Nut Island), or Penang, George Town is the island's main attraction and a UNESCO World Heritage Site. With rich colonial and historic roots amid the clutter of a market and commercial town, its narrow streets and busy thoroughfares add to the adventure. The city's Chinese history is reflected in the shophouses and old hotels, and it also offers delicious food and great shopping.

Most of Penang's activity is in the city, but it is also possible to relax at a beach-side resort or to flee the heat by taking the railway link to the top of Bukit Bendera (Penang Hill). While George Town is predominantly Chinese, the western part of the island is rural Malay countryside with fruit orchards and quaint fishing villages.

Entry points to the island are by road and rail, a ferry journey across the Selat Selatan from the industrial town of Seberangi Prai or by way of the 7km (4.5-mile) drive over the Penang Bridge, which provides wonderful views of the harbour. South of this bridge is the Second Penang Bridge (due to be completed late 2013) linking Batu Maung with Batu Kawan on the mainland. Flights, including international

The Penang State Legislative Building in George Town

arrivals, land at the Bayan Lepas International Airport, which is 18km (11 miles) south of George Town.

Under the British, Penang was named Prince of Wales Island, and the capital took its name from the son of King George III. Nowadays, Penang has the second-largest economy among the states of Malaysia, and a population of over 1.6 million. It is also the centre for the country's electronics industry.

George Town

There are many ways to discover this historic city – by foot, trishaw or bicycle – but do wear a hat and sunblock and drink plenty of water.

Colonial Heritage Walk

One of the joys of touring George Town's historic section is the opportunity to cover many of the sites in this compact area by foot, and the best place to begin your tour is the main ferry terminal at **Weld Quay**. Along the foreshore there are the **Clan Jetties**, a hamlet of houses on stilts, joined by wooden walkways over the water and inhabited by 2,000 boatmen and fishing families, each group belonging to a different Chinese clan.

At the other end of Pengkalan Weld is the **Jam Besar** (Clock Tower), presented to the town in 1897 to mark Queen Victoria's Diamond Jubilee.

Across the road is **Fort Cornwallis** (named after Charles Cornwallis, Governor General of India), which marks the spot where Captain Francis Light arrived on 17 July 1786. The greenery of the park and gardens surrounds the fortifications, which were originally made of wood and rebuilt in 1810. Light's statue stands inside the entrance of the fort. As no photograph of Light existed, the sculpture is a likeness made from a portrait of his son, William (who founded the city of Adelaide in South Australia).

Jalan Tun Syed Sheh Barakbah (also known as the Esplanade) runs between the waterfront and the Padang before the fort. This area is lined with handsome, 19th-century colonial government buildings and their brilliant white is highly evocative of the era in which they were built. The British worshipped in **St George's Church** (1818) on Lebuh Farquhar. It is the oldest Anglican church in Southeast Asia. In the nearby Protestant cemetery, set among frangipani trees, is the **grave of Francis Light**, who died from malaria in 1794, only eight years after the start of his Penang adventure. The tombstones of many other graves reveal the hardships of the town's history.

The **Penang Museum and Art Gallery** on Lebuh Farquhar is housed in what was the Penang Free School (1816), the first English-language school in Southeast Asia. There is a fine collection of historical memorabilia, old paintings, etchings and a 19th-century Chinese bridal chamber.

Clearing the forest

On the northeast corner of the waterfront, Kedah Point marks the spot where the Penang settlement's founder Francis Light (see page 21) is said to have hit upon a cunning method of getting the surrounding forest cleared to make way for the town. He loaded a cannon with Spanish silver dollars, fired them into the forest, and invited local labourers to hack their way through the undergrowth to get to the money.

Cheong Fatt Tze Mansion

One of the great monuments from George Town's colonial days is the **Eastern & Oriental Hotel** at 10 Lebuh Farquhar. Even if you are not staying in one of the hotel's grand old rooms – where Rudyard Kipling and Somerset Maugham both stayed – have a drink in the venerable Farquhar's Bar, overlooking the harbour, which is always lined with vessels from around the world. The E & O is actually a fusion of two separate hotels: the Eastern, facing the Esplanade, and the Oriental, facing the sea. It was the brainchild of Martin and Tigran Sharkie, Armenian brothers who also created the famous Raffles Hotel in Singapore.

Nanyang Heritage Sites

This trail will bring you round to visit houses that display late 19th century Nanyang (South Seas) Chinese architecture and decorative arts. The **Cheong Fatt Tze Mansion** on Lebuh Leith, built around 1860 by Thio Thaw Siat, a Chinese businessman, is considered one of the best examples of 19th-century Chinese architecture in Penang. Restored to its former glory, this 38-room, five-courtyard house gained UNESCO recognition in 2000 and is now a boutique hotel. Tours are conducted three times a day for a small fee.

The **Pinang Peranakan Museum** on Lebuh Gereja is a mansion built by millionaire Chung Keng Kwee, but today holds a wide collection of jewellery, costumes and antique furniture of the Chinese Peranakan (the Baba Nyonya), descendants of Chinese settlers who adopted certain Malay ways.

Street of Harmony Walk

The busiest public temple in Penang is the **Kuan Yin Temple**, on Jalan Masjid Kapitan Keling, near St George's Church. Dedicated to the Goddess of Mercy, who is identified with the Indian Boddhisattva of Fertility, it draws both the rich and poor to pay respect and is popular with newly wed couples. The atmosphere is heavy with the scent of burning joss sticks mixed with the aroma of flowers, scented oils, fruits, cakes and roast chicken, offered on the altars to help solve family problems.

On the same street is the **Masjid Kapitan Keling**, the state's oldest mosque, built in 1800 for Muslim Indian soldiers. The **Sri Maha Mariamman Temple** on Lebuh Queen was built in 1883 and is the oldest Hindu temple in Penang. Vividly decorated, it is dedicated to Lord Subramaniam, the son of Shiva and destroyer of evil, who is the focus of worship during the Thaipusam festival held in the early months of the year.

Historic Enclave Walk

The small enclave bordered by Lebuh Armenian in the north, Lebuh Cannon in the east and Lebuh Acheh in

Clan associations

Chinese immigrants arriving in Malaysia in the 19th century fell under the protection and control of clan associations, similar in function to medieval European guilds.

The Khoo Kongsi in George Town

the southwest is the meeting point of Confucian and Islamic civilisations. **No. 120 Lebuh Armenian** was the Penang headquarters of the Tongmenghui, the political party of the Chinese leader Dr Sun Yat-Sen; the ground floor is open to the public and there is a short video presentation. On Lebuh Acheh the **George Town World Heritage Office** has tourist information about the city.

The more flamboyant residential houses are the **Clan Houses**, bulwarks of community solidarity. Clan houses combine temples for ancestral worship with meeting halls to settle local problems – housing, jobs, medical care, help for orphans and discreetly handled intra-community crime. Off Lebuh Cannon – so called because of the holes made in the road surface here by cannonballs fired during the Great Penang Riot of 1867 – and through a laneway is the **Khoo Kongsi** (clan house of the family Khoo). Approach it via a narrow alley near the intersection of Lebuh Acheh and Jalan Masjid Kapitan

Keling. Inside is an image of the clan's patron, Tua Sai Yeah, a renowned general of the Ch'in dynasty (221–207BC). Other houses nearby date back to the mid-19th century. The ornate ancestral temple **Leong San Tong** stands opposite a smaller hall used for open-air Chinese opera and theatre. To the left is a shrine to the God of Prosperity and to the right is the hall of *sinchoo* (soul-tablets), gold plaques honouring clan dignitaries and simpler wooden panels for more humble clan members.

Southwest of George Town

The other main sights of interest outside George Town are Penang Hill and the Botanical Gardens. The drive out along **Jalan Sultan Ahmad Shah** takes you past the rubber magnates' huge neo-Gothic and Palladian mansions, built during the boom that lasted through World War I.

The Buddhist **Wat Chaiyamangkalaram** monastery, on Lorong Burma, is famous for its reclining Buddha, 33m (108ft) long. Queen Victoria gave the site for the temple to the community in 1845.

Further west, away from the temple, you'll find the **Penang Botanic Gardens**. The 30-hectare (74-acre) garden was created in 1844 as a tribute to Charles Curtis, its superintendent, who collected botanical specimens from the nearby hills. Leaf monkeys and long-tailed macaques are among the wildlife.

Jalan Dato Keramat, then Jalan Air Itam, leads west from the town to **Suffolk House,** where a guided tour introduces you to the Anglo-Indian garden house on the pepper estate once owned by Francis Light. Continue west to **Penang Hill**, 833m (2,733ft) above sea level, which served as a colonial hill station in the early 20th century. Take a five-minute ride on the Penang Hill Railway past bungalows and villas set amid tropical gardens for panoramic views of the island. Birdwatchers should look out for blue-tailed bee-eaters, sunbirds and spider-hunters.

Above the small town of Air Itam stands the **Kek Lok Si** (Temple of Paradise). It was founded by Abbot Beow Lean, a Chinese Buddhist priest from Fujian Province in China who arrived in Penang in 1887. The temple's construction began in 1890 and took 20 years to complete. The centrepiece is the seven-tiered **Pagoda of a Million Buddhas**, which is 30m (98ft) high and dedicated to Tsi Tsuang Wang. The pagoda is actually a blend of three architectural styles, a Chinese octagonal base, a Thai central core and a Burmese peak. Inside the shrine are statues of the Laughing Buddha, radiating happiness; Sakyamuni Buddha, incarnation of the faith's founder; and Kuan Yin, the Goddess of Mercy.

Western Penang island
Away from George Town's hectic, bustling streets and midday heat, there is the chance to explore the remainder of the island.

Strolling along Batu Ferringi beach

Head to **Balik Pulau** town and join a cycling tour to see the Malays, who live largely in the rural *kampungs* and fishing villages. The landscape here is a blend of hilly rainforest and occasional plantations of rubber, oil palms, pepper, nutmeg, cloves and other spices. This part of the island can be toured in a day – overnight accommodation away from the beach resorts and George Town is limited.

Meromictic lake

Penang National Park has one of two natural meromictic lakes in Asia. Off Pantai Kerachut, the lake is seasonal, filling up with seawater and freshwater only during the monsoon months (April–May and Oct–Nov). Being meromictic, the two layers of water never intermix because of different densities.

Northwest of George Town

About 15km (9 miles) northwest of George Town are the resorts of **Batu Ferringi,** with sandy beaches and rows of luxury resorts offering waterskiing, sailing, windsurfing, horse riding and other sports. There are also small hotels for travellers on a budget. Be aware that water sports accidents have occurred there and the beaches may disappoint those who have travelled elsewhere in Malaysia.

Alternatively, you could trek through the **Penang National Park**. The forest reserve covers some 20 sq km (8 sq miles) of the island's northwest corner. With only camping available as accommodation and vehicles denied access, the reward comes in possible sightings of wildlife like wild pigs, leopard-cats, slow loris, flying lemurs, leaf monkeys, macaques and black squirrels. The landscape is dotted with granite outcrops.

Near Teluk Bahang's town centre are the **Tropical Spice Garden** and **Penang Cultural Centre**; the latter features art, crafts, music and dance, as well as traditional architecture from elsewhere in Malaysia. At the southern end of Teluk

Kedah is the country's rice basket

Bahang village is the **Penang Butterfly Farm**, which has hundreds of different specimens fluttering around a netted enclosure of landscaped gardens.

A **tropical fruit farm**, just 8km (5 miles) from Teluk Bahang, has cultivated 140 types of exotic fruit trees on its 10 hectares (25 acres) since opening in 1992.

Kedah

From Seberangi Prai the road stretches north into **Kedah** state and heads into the rice bowl of Malaysia. The archaeological site at **Lembah Bujang** (Bujang Valley) ❻ possibly dates back to a 5th-century Hindu kingdom called Langkasuka, which Indian traders may have used as an entrepôt with China. Buddhist temples have also been uncovered in the area. Via the towns of Sungai Petani and Bedong, a left turn takes you to **Merbok** to visit the **Candi Bukit Batu Pahat** (Temple of Chiselled Stone Hill). This is one of the 10th-century temples now reconstructed in the Lembah Bujang and possibly built by representatives of the South Indian Pallava dynasty before the 7th century BC. More artefacts, ceramics, *lingams* (phallic symbols), stone caskets, and gold and silver Shiva symbols are on show at Merbok's **Muzium Arkeologi Lembah Bujang (Lembah Bujang Archaeological Museum)**.

Beyond the highest peak in Kedah, 1,200m (3,936ft) Gunung Jerai, lie rice fields fed by Sungai Muda. These extend northeast to Tasik Muda (Lake Muda), the gateway to the **Ulu Muda Forest Reserve**, which is accessible only by boat. This remote rainforest, with basic accommodation, gives visitors a chance to spot elephants, hornbills and maybe even the elusive tiger.

In the city centre of the Kedah state capital **Alor Setar** is the traditional *padang* (square), dominated by the Crown of Kedah monument. The **Masjid Zahir**, built in 1912, stands on the square's western side. The **Muzium Negeri** (State Museum), about 15 minutes by car just north of the city, was built in 1736, and is worth a visit for its collection of *Bunga Mas* and *Bunga Perak* (flowers made of real gold and silver), sent to the ancient court of Siam as tribute.

The nearby port of **Kuala Kedah** is a departure point for ferries to Langkawi; you can see the remains of an 18th-century fort and sample some of Malaysia's best seafood.

Pulau Langkawi

Part of an archipelago of some 99 islands, the delightful resort island of **Langkawi** ❼ is Southeast Asia's first UNESCO Geopark and lies just south of the sea border with Thailand. With its numerous hotels and resorts, it is increasingly seen as Malaysia's premier island destination.

For those travelling by road (rather than flying from KL), ferries leave from Kuala Perlis and Kuala Kedah. There are daily ferries from Penang and several per day to Satun in southern

Langkawi Geopark

Langkawi's geological formations have been evolving for more than 550 million years. Besides the three geoforest parks at Machinchang, Kilim and Dayang Bunting, there are also four geological monuments and 10 protected geosites, covering islands, waterfalls, lakes, ancient fossils, pinnacles, caves and beaches. These fossils of ancient and extinct sea creatures, between 550 and 250 million years, old are remarkably preserved in the rock and limestone landscape, but they are easier to find at Kilim.

Langkawi's SkyBridge

Thailand. There are also flights to Langkawi from Singapore.

For ferry travellers, the **Jetty Point Duty-free Complex** in **Kuah** is your arrival point, while those coming by air will land at the international airport, 18km (11 miles) northwest of the town. Kuah has some good Chinese, Thai, Indian and Malay restaurants and shops selling a range of goods at duty-free prices. Kuah's town square is dominated by a sculpture of a giant eagle (*langkawi* means red eagle in Malay).

It is possible to explore Langkawi's 80km (50 miles) of roads by hiring a car, but many find motorcycles and scooters a better and cheaper alternative to reach parts of the island. South of Kuah is Pulau Tuba and Pulau Dayang Bunting, which make up the **Dayang Bunting Marble Geoforest Park**. This area and two other parts of the island form a geopark that protects the rocks, plants and animals. You can swim in **Tasik Dayang Bunting** (Lake of the Pregnant Maiden), Langkawi's largest freshwater lake, associated with the fable of a Kedah princess who drank the lake's water and became pregnant. Just be mindful of the aggressive food-pinching monkeys in the area.

Most resort and budget accommodation is located around **Pantai Cenang** and **Pantai Tengah** on the island's southwestern tip, within easy reach of the international airport. Here you will also find the island's best public beaches. Elsewhere on the island, the fine beaches at **Burau Bay**, **Datai Bay** and **Tanjung Rhu** are reserved for the exclusive use of hotel guests.

Underwater World Langkawi at Pantai Cenang is reputed to be the largest aquarium in Southeast Asia, with over 5,000 marine and freshwater species. Nearby is the **Muzium Laman Padi** (Rice Garden Museum), which explains how rice is planted and harvested. En route to the airport is **Temple Tree at Bon Ton,** a collection of heritage homes that were once in a state of sore neglect and scattered around the peninsular. Each house was relocated here in pieces and reassembled as luxury accommodation. Also nearby the airport, the **Pisang Handicraft & Art Village** showcases batik artists at work.

Head northwest to the **Machinchang Cambrian Geoforest Park** to visit the **Langkawi Geopark Tourist Information Centre** at the Oriental Village shopping complex. Here you can get an insight into how geologically different the three geoforest parks are. Ride the **Panorama Langkawi** to the top of the 708m (2,320ft) Gunung Machinchang and cross the gravity-defying **SkyBridge**. Plan to be here at sunset to appreciate the best panoramas of the Andaman Sea and Thailand from the viewing platforms.

On the northern coast of Langkawi, on Jalan Teluk Yu, is the **Kompleks Kraf Langkawi** handicraft centre. But a more worthwhile reason to stop is for the **Customs and Wedding Museum,** showcasing the traditions of Malaysia's ethnic groups.

Cruise boats depart from Kilim Jetty to tour the **Kilim Karst Geoforest Park**, in northeastern Langkawi. But the best way to see these majestic limestone hills and mangrove forests is to paddle your own **kayak** through the narrow channels of brackish water. Besides the wildlife – soaring Brahminy Kites, mischievous macaques and languid snakes – there is also a visit to **Gua Kelawar,** a small cave populated by fruit bats. Nearby, on Jalan Ayer Hangat, retired Dr Ghani Hussain

A small cruising boat off Langkawi

regales visitors (including two of Malaysia's former premiers) on his **Herbwalk** about the medicinal properties of some of his plants. His collection includes more than 600 species.

South of Langkawi is the marine park of **Pulau Payar,** where underwater visibility is rarely more than 3m (10ft), but there is nevertheless lots of life, including baby black-tip reef sharks and colourful soft coral blooms on wrecks in deeper waters.

Perlis

Malaysia's smallest state, **Perlis**, also marks a change of scenery, from the flat rice lands to solitary limestone outcrops, many containing subterranean caves. The main towns are **Arau**, the royal town, and **Padang Besar**, where the Malaysian and Thai railways meet. An alternative route into Thailand is via the **Perlis State Park,** where, for the adventurous, a visit to the **Gua Wang Burma** is recommended (prior booking is required). From **Kuala Perlis**, south of the state capital,

Kangar, it is a 45-minute ferry ride to Langkawi and there are regular departures during the day.

THE EAST COAST AND INTERIOR

Malaysia's less-visited east coast offers visitors a slower pace, set against the beauty of the region's beaches and the richness of its forests. The region covers three states – **Kelantan**, **Terengganu** and **Pahang** – with most road traffic plying the coastal road between Kota Bharu, close to the Thai border, and Kuala Rompin in the south, the gateway to the Pahang section of the Endau-Rompin State Park. Historically resistant to many of the major changes in the rest of Malaysia, the region has been able to maintain its authentic Malay culture (with some Thai influence in northern Kelantan) and Islamic traditions.

The east coast's beaches are less developed and offer opportunities for snorkelling and diving. Further into the interior, wildlife enthusiasts can enter the forests in Taman Negara National Park from all three states for jungle trekking and adventure travel. Kenyir and Bera are two large freshwater lakes for angling aficionados and at Tasik Bera visitors can also experience life with the Orang Asli from the Semelai tribe.

The region also offers the chance to see leatherback turtles coming to lay their eggs at Cherating near Kuantan; and to view the artisans at Kuala Terengganu, whose boat-building skills are legendary.

Kelantan

White sandy beaches stretch north from the state capital, **Kota Bharu**, to the Thai border. Buddhist temples close to the capital hark back to the time when Kelantan

Kampung crafts

Traditional handicrafts, including the making of spinning tops, kites, silverware, baskets and batik, are still practised in many of the rural *kampung* in Kelantan and Terengganu.

A fisherman with his *Bangau* boat at Bachok Beach

was under the influence of Siamese kings. The British colonial influence here, which came into being in a 1909 agreement with Siam, lasted only three decades before defeat by the Japanese in World War II. Kelantan's isolation, as well as its embrace of Islam in the 17th century, enabled this cradle of Malay culture to remain intact.

Here you will see soaring decorative kites as well as the *wayang kulit* (shadow puppet shows), dating back to when Kelantan was influenced by the kingdom of Funan in Indochina some 2,000 years ago.

Known as the 'Land of Lightning' – due to the heavy storms during the wet season of November to February – Kelantan's gateway is Kota Bharu, just 40 minutes by air from Kuala Lumpur and only 30km (19 miles) from the Thai border. To the south, where towns dot the main highway, are points of access to the many beaches and fishing villages that are at the heart of the region's economy and culture.

Kota Bharu

On the banks of the Kelantan River, Kota Bharu's key attractions are close to the **Pasar Besar Siti Khadijah** (Central Market) on Jalan Hulu. Here rows of food and farm produce resemble works of art, with vegetables, fruit and meat on the ground level and kitchenware, baskets and other goods on the floors above.

The **Buluh Kubu Bazaar** is good for bargain-hunters seeking T-shirts or silverware. Cottage-industry goods are found over the Jalan Wakaf Mek Zainab bridge, while the **night market**, near Pasar Besar, provides worthwhile evening entertainment and gives visitors a chance to savour Kelantanese food.

At sundown, riverside restaurants also come to life near to **Padang Merdeka** (Independence Square). The square was the site where the body of slain Malay warrior Tok Janggut (Father Long Beard), who led a rebellion against the British in the early years of the century, was exhibited in 1915. The Declaration of Independence was read here on 31 August 1957.

Across the square on Jalan Sultan is the state's first brick building, a bank used by the Japanese Army as their headquarters during World War II but now the **Memorial Perang Bank Kerapu**, a war memorial museum. Next door is the **Muzium Islam** (Islamic Museum), and the ornate **Masjid Al-Muhammadi** (State Mosque) beyond.

The **Istana Jahar** (Museum of Royal Traditions and Customs) was built in 1887, with additions by Sultan Muhammad IV in the early years of the 20th century. The **Istana Balai Besar** (Palace with the Great Hall) was built in 1840 under Sultan Muhammad II and is now open only on ceremonial occasions (for invited guests). The best glimpse of living Malaysian culture can be seen at the **Gelanggang Seni** (Cultural Centre), on Jalan Mahmood opposite the Perdana Hotel. Performances here include *wayang kulit*, *main gasing* (top spinning) and *silat* (selfdefence), except on Fridays and during Ramadan. For the latest performance schedules, visit the Tourism Malaysia office on the ground floor of **Kampung Kraftangan** (Handicraft Village), 2km (1.2 miles) southwest from here.

Around Kota Bharu

Within just a few kilometres of Kota Bharu, visitors can find master silversmiths and expert batik-makers, but the maze of country lanes around the town could make it difficult to find the *kampung* communities where the artisans still use their traditional skills. The Tourist Information Centre on Jalan Sultan Ibrahim can recommend a guide.

Silver-craft factories can be visited at **Kampung Sireh**, along Jalan Sultanah Zainab, **Kampung Marak** and **Kampung Badang**, as well as on the road to Pantai Cahaya Bulan (PCB). Also on the way to PCB, visitors can see the skill and beauty of *kain songket*, richly woven materials of gold and silver thread, at **Kampung Penambang**. *Songket* was the product of the region's early trade with China (silk) and India (gold and silver thread). Batik-makers are found throughout the state, but there are bigger factories at **Kampung Puteh**, **Kubur Kuda** and **Kampung Badang,** near the city.

Kite-makers also practise their age-old skills throughout the region, and while tradition would have the art passed from father to son, many fear the younger generation now lacks the patience to carry out the skilled handiwork required.

One of the oldest mosques in Malaysia is at **Nilam Puri**. Masjid Kampung Laut was dismantled and taken from a site closer to the river at Kampung Laut in 1968, after repeated flooding. The mosque was built entirely without the use of nails. It is now a centre for religious studies and open only to Muslims.

Kelantan's ancient links with Thailand are evident in the number of Thai Buddhist Temples you will see half-hidden among the groves of palm and laurel,

Temple attire

When visiting a place of worship remember to dress in an appropriately dignified manner. Note that you must also take off your shoes before entering a Hindu temple or a mosque rising above the rice paddies. North of the estuary of the Kelantan River near **Tumpat** (12km/7 miles from town) is one of the most important of these temples, **Wat Phothivihan**, noted for its 40m (130ft) reclining Buddha. At **Kampung Perasit**, south of Kota Bharu, is **Wat Putharamaram**.

A significant landmark of World War II can be visited at **Sabak Beach**, 13km (8 miles) northwest of Kota Bharu, near the mouth of the Kelantan River. Here is the site of the first Japanese assault in the Pacific War, just over an hour before Pearl Harbor was bombed. Jutting out of the sandy

A craftsman making *wau* in Kota Bharu

beach in the pleasant shade of palm and casuarina trees stands a crumbling bunker that the Indian artillery defended to the last soldier.

The Beaches

Kelantan's white sandy beaches are easily reached from Kota Bharu and provide plenty of opportunities for a pleasant swim. Most popular is **Pantai Cahaya Bulan**, or Moonlight Beach. It is 10km (6 miles) north of the town, one reason why it is so popular during weekends and holidays.

Pantai Seri Tujuh (Beach of the Seven Lagoons), about 7km (4 miles) from Kota Bharu, lies on the border with Thailand.

Snorkelling off Pulau
Perhentian Besar

To the south, **Pantai Irama** (Melody Beach) is some 25km (16 miles) from Kota Bharu; it is one of the most beautiful along the entire coast. On the journey to Terengganu is **Pantai Bisikan Bayu** (Beach of the Whispering Breeze, also known as Pantai Dalam Rhu). Stop off at the fishing village of **Semerak**, 19km (12 miles) from Pasir Puteh, where you can buy excellent seafood for a barbecue on the beach.

South of PCB is the **Gunung Stong State Park,** where you can trek, with the assistance of a guide, to the impressive seven-tier **Jelawang Waterfall**, one of the highest falls in Malaysia, and camp nearby.

Terengganu

A coast of sandy beaches along the 225km (140 miles) of landfall facing the South China Sea, not to mention several offshore islands and hinterland forests near Tasik (Lake) Kenyir, give Terengganu its appeal. The wealth from offshore oil discoveries in recent years has buoyed the state, something you'll see reflected in the skyline and busy traffic of the capital, Kuala Terengganu. So far the economic gains have failed to detract from the town's relaxed charm. The main options for travelling to Terengganu are direct flights from KL or interstate buses to Kuala Terengganu, which is generally the starting point for a trip to the island resorts or to Tasik Kenyir.

The Islands

The islands off Terengganu's north coast are accessible from both Kuala Terengganu or by way of the fishing village of **Kuala Besut**, 45km (28 miles) south of Kota Bharu,

which is the departure point to Pulau Perhentian's **islands ❽**.

These islands of **Pulau Perhentian Kecil** and **Pulau Perhentian Besar** are reached after a 45-minute speedboat ride. Their main appeal is that they are lush and tropical, with clear blue waters and coral reefs protected as part of Malaysia's marine park network. On both islands, accommodation ranges from good resorts to chalets.

South from Pulau Perhentian Besar lies **Pulau Redang**, some 50km (31 miles) off the coast, and if snorkelling or diving you may get to see green turtles in the surrounding seas. **Pasir Panjang** (Long Beach) has the most bars and clubs, and is known for its party atmosphere. The journey to the islands takes two hours from the village of **Merang** (not to be confused with the town of **Marang** further south). There are also resorts on **Pulau Lang Tengah**, just west of the Redang Islands. Boats take 45 minutes to reach the island from Merang.

Kuala Terengganu

The lively state capital of **Kuala Terengganu**, bordered by the Terengganu River and the South China Sea, is the largest town in the state and has progressed from a sleepy fishing village to a bustling, colourful centre. Aside from the beautiful **Masjid Tengku Tengah Zaharah**, 4.5km (3 miles) out of town, most sites of interest are along the town's waterfront. The mosque, built on an estuary of the Ibai River, gives the illusion that it is floating on water.

Back in town, a waterfront stroll leads through **Chinatown,** on Jalan Bandar. The old terraced buildings on both sides of the road create an attractive sense of timelessness even as the betting shops do a lively afternoon trade. Jalan Bandar leads you to the **Pasar Besar Kedai Payang** (Central Market), a multi-level complex attached to a car park, with a fruit, vegetable and fish market on the ground floor and local textiles and handicrafts above.

A short river cruise from the jetty, **Pulau Duyong** is a little island of boat-builders, whose reputations extend far beyond Malaysia. Late in the year, the Monsoon Cup sailing race is staged off the island in the blustery monsoon breezes.

Several other attractions are located outside the town. Opposite Pulau Sekati, 5km (3 miles) from town – but also accessible via the river – is the **Terengganu State Museum,** in a traditionally styled complex of four blocks housing 10 galleries at Bukit Losong. The largest state museum in Malaysia, its galleries are dedicated to maritime exhibits, traditional architecture, Islamic arts, textiles, crafts and royal regalia. For local silk weaving, try the **Sutera Semai Centre** at Chendering, 6km (3 miles) from Kuala Terengganu, where visitors can see different stages of silk-making and batik-painting. Also on offer is *songket*, woven with silver and gold threads, and brassware.

Around Kuala Terengganu

Around 55km (34 miles) inland from Kuala Terengganu is the largest constructed lake in Southeast Asia, **Tasik Kenyir ❾**. It was created by flooding the valley to make the country's largest hydroelectric dam, completed in 1985. For anglers looking for freshwater fish, the waters of Tasik Kenyir, covering an area of 260,000 hectares (642,460 acres) and 340 islands, are the place to go. There is also an adventurous trail to Taman Negara. Besides fishing, jet-skiing, windsurfing, canoeing and jungle trekking are also available.

There are also several waterfalls, rapids and cascades within the lake region, including the **Sekayu Waterfall**, just 56km (35 miles) west of Kuala Terengganu. After trekking through the rainforest, you can enjoy a swim in one of the many natural pools created among the rocks by the cascading river.

Marang is a fishing village 15km (9 miles) south of Kuala Terengganu. It provides access to the island of **Pulau Kapas** which, though less than 2km (1 mile) in length, is considered one of

Tasik Kenyir

the finest islands on the east coast. There are several resorts and chalet accommodation on the island.

Rantau Abang

Turtle-watching at **Rantau Abang** was once the cornerstone of tourism in Terengganu. The Turtle and Marine Ecosystem Centre here released around half a million hatchlings between 1975 and 2005. However, while all four turtle species found in the state are protected, in 2011 no leatherback turtle landed to lay eggs at Rantau Abang, although there were a few the year before.

The dramatic decline in nesting turtles over the past decade has inevitably led to a drop in tourists visiting Rantau Abang, but there was renewed hope with the establishment

Sekayu Waterfall

of the **Ma'Daerah Turtle Sanctuary**, 10km (6 miles) north of Kemaman. Under the management of the Department of Fisheries, the sanctuary provides hatchery facilities on the beach between the towns of Kerteh and Paka. It is a restricted area and not open to visitors unless they have written permission.

Kuala Dungun and Points South

The highway south from Rantau Abang, heading towards Kuantan, the state capital of Pahang, passes through **Kuala Dungun**, which is predominantly Chinese in character and offers excellent cuisine. From here you can hire a boat to the island of **Pulau Tenggol**, 30km (18 miles) offshore, where you can go swimming and snorkelling among the angelfish. The centre of Terengganu's petroleum industry is **Kerteh**, with its refineries and gasworks. But there are some picturesque beaches at the mouth of the Kerteh River nonetheless.

Pahang

The largest state in the peninsula has the longest river, the 475km (296-mile) long Pahang. Although its most famous sights lie to the west in the Genting and Cameron Highlands, Pahang has island resorts including the renowned Pulau Tioman (Tioman Island) in the far south (though access by sea is from Mersing in Johor). Endau-Rompin National Park, straddling the border with Johor state, complements the better-known Taman Negara in the far north, which has road access through the state capital Kuantan. Tasik Bera is a scenic lake, and visitors can also stay with the Orang Asli of the Semelai tribe.

The Coast

Just 47km (30 miles) from Kuantan is the beach resort areas of **Cherating**, **Balok Beach** and **Pantai Teluk Chempedak**, the latter 5km (3 miles) out of the bustling city. The beautiful **Pelindung Beach** is just a short trek through the Teluk

Save the turtles

In the years before ecological awareness, many onlookers treated the turtles' rendezvous as a popular spectacle. Crowds gathered in festive mood to build campfires on the beach, dance to loud music, take pictures by blinding flashlight of the turtles' night-time egg laying, even ride the backs of the leatherback turtles. This irresponsibility almost put a stop to the natural phenomenon. The annual number of leatherbacks visiting Rantau Abang declined from about 2,000 in the 1950s to barely a few hundred by the end of the 1980s. At this point, the Malaysian Fisheries Department stepped in. Authorities have banned the use of flash photography or flashlights, discouraged people from consuming turtle eggs, and visitors must stay 5m (15ft) from the turtles. Despite this, in 2010, only a handful of leatherback turtles landed to lay 10 eggs at Rantau Abang and in 2011 there were none.

Chempedak Forest Reserve. From May to September, green turtles may be seen under moonlit skies when they lay their eggs on the beach. You will find a pleasant beach nearby at **Batu Hitam**.

Kuantan

Kuantan offers a wide range of hotels, a lively shopping and market quarter, and a quiet ambience next to the river where good food stalls are found. Built on the fortunes from tin mining, the capital is now a commercial centre for Pahang's oil, palm and other industries, and a key link in the east coast petroleum and gas pipelines.

Jalan Masjid is where you will find the state mosque of **Masjid Sultan Ahmad Shah** and the **Tourist Information Centre**. The area around Jalan Haji Abdul Aziz and Jalan Besar has many shops, warehouses and the occasional moneylender. The nearby village of **Selamat,** at the estuary of Sungai Galing, is known for its fine *kain songket* silk brocade.

Sungai Lembing

About 42km (26 miles) northwest from Kuantan is the small tin-mining town of **Sungai Lembing**, which once had the most extensive subterranean mines in the world. Today it is the gateway to the **Rainbow Waterfall**, where a gorgeous rainbow at the base of the falls greets visitors who arrive well before 11am. If fine weather prevails, allow for a two-hour journey by four-wheel-drive and on foot to see this natural phenomenon. The town also has an informative **Muzium Sungai Lembing** housed in the former mine manager's bungalow atop a hill overlooking the town. For a taste of local cuisine, dine at the food court at the **Pasar Sungai Lembing**.

Pekan

The sleepy old royal capital of Pahang, 45km (28 miles) south of Kuantan, is home to the sultan's palace, **Istana Abu Bakar**,

In Kuantan's Masjid Sultan Ahmad Shah

set upstream on the Pahang River among immaculate polo fields. Gilded and sapphire-blue domes grace two marble mosques and the **Sultan's Mausoleum**. Nearby, on Jalan Sultan Ahmad, is the Victorian **State Museum (Muzium Sultan Abu Bakar)** that displays glories of the old sultanate and treasures from a Chinese junk salvaged from the South China Sea. The town also has a silk-weaving centre at the **Pulau Keladi Cultural Village**, 5km (3 miles) from Pekan.

Lanchang

Near the town of Lanchang, 178km (111 miles) west of Pekan, is the **Kuala Gandah Elephant Sanctuary,** where visitors can interact with the endangered Asian elephant. Any visitor can feed the elephants from 2pm onwards, but only the first 100 who arrive at 1pm can ride and help bathe the elephants. However, as the sanctuary relies on visitors to minimise its operating expenses, do expect to see

In Kuala Gandah Elephant Sanctuary

elephants put on a show for the tourists.

Taman Negara

The national park of **Taman Negara** ⑩ provides an ideal setting for exploring vast rainforest, fast-flowing rivers and mountains of the peninsula's Main Range. It covers an area of 4,343 sq km (1,676 sq miles), spreading across three states: Pahang, Terengganu and Kelantan.

Backpackers may want to go it alone, but most people are advised to plan their visit through a tour operator. Armed with an entry permit, visitors head first to the park headquarters, about 101km (63 miles) northeast of Lanchang by road via Jerantut and 60km (37 miles) by motor-powered longboat from Kuala Tembeling.

The **boat ride** on the Tembeling River is likely to be one of the highlights of your visit. Along the way, you may see wildlife and the Orang Asli fishermen – the only human residents allowed by park authorities to stay here. Wear a hat and bring along plenty of bottled water. The journey usually takes about three hours; even longer when short stretches of the river dry up, occasionally forcing passengers to walk along the riverbank while the boatmen push the sampan through the shallows.

You can also choose to take a two-hour drive from Jerantut to Kampung Kuala Tahan (village) where budget accommodation, convenience stores and floating restaurants serving local and Western cuisine are available. On the riverbank opposite the village is the headquarters at **Kuala Tahan**, which has a good range of accommodation, from resort chalets to bungalows and a dormitory, plus a restaurant and a general store. The park headquarters organises informative evening slide-shows as a general introduction to the features of the rainforest.

Forest Trails

There are marked trails leading from the park's headquarters into the forest, which you can explore with your own group or on an organised tour. There are both day trips and overnight tours to observation hides, where you can watch for wildlife visiting nearby salt licks and watering holes. Overnight stays are organised at several observation hides (*bumbun*), namely at **Kumbang**, **Yong**, **Tabing**, **Belau** and **Cegar Anjing**. Park headquarters will provide sheets if you do not have a sleeping bag. The most popular walk is across the elevated canopy trail, 27m (80ft) above the ground. From park headquarters, day trips leaving in the early morning include a walk to Bukit Indah, followed by a boat ride through the rapids to **Kuala Trenggan**, returning to headquarters on foot; a walk to the **Tabing Hide**, followed by a boat ride to the **Lata Berkoh** rapids, then another trek back to headquarters; a boat ride on the Tembeling River to the **Gua Telinga** (Bat Cave), which you enter on hands and knees until you can stand. You then find yourself in a great vault inhabited by hundreds of fruit and insect-eating bats, which have little interest in humans. Only the squeamish will object to the giant toads and harmless little white cave-racer snakes.

The most adventurous trek for experienced walkers and climbers is a seven to nine-day walk up and down the peninsula's highest peak, **Gunung Tahan** (2,187m/7,175ft). A jungle guide must accompany the group on the strenuous climb.

Flora and Fauna

The dipterocarp rainforest here includes the tualang tree. At 50m (164ft), it is the tallest tree in Southeast Asia. At heights above 1,500m (5,000ft), you will see montane trees from the oak and laurel families.

With patience and luck by day, or rotating shift watches by night, you may see wild pigs, sambars, barking deer, gibbons, pig-tailed macaques, leaf monkeys, tree shrews or flying squirrels. Visitors to the **Kumbang Hide** have sometimes even caught sight of rare tigers and leopards.

During the fruit season, birdwatchers have spotted up to 70 species just around the park headquarters. Among them are lesser fish eagles, crested serpent eagles, fireback pheasants and garnet pittas. From September to March you can also see migrant Arctic warblers, Japanese paradise flycatchers and Siberian blue robins.

The view of Taman Negara National Park from Teresek Hill

Even if you do not spot much of the wildlife mentioned here – and you are bound to see something – the sheer experience of the forest at night, with its incredible noises, the flitting of mysteri-

ous fireflies and the sense of invisible but omnipresent life and movement around you, will make it all worthwhile.

Tasik Bera

About 129km (80 miles) south of Jerantut is **Tasik Bera**. Protected under the RAMSAR Convention as a wetland of international importance, the lake and the surrounding forests is home to the Orang Asli of the **Semelai tribe**, as well as a wealth of biodiversity. Spend time with the Semelai to learn how they depend on the lake and forests to sustain them and to experience the centuries-old cultural traditions they practise to this day.

Pulau Tioman

The combination of first-rate resort facilities and magnificent natural beauty makes **Pulau Tioman** one of the finest in Asia. Preserved from logging, most of the rainforest has remained. A hilly ridge runs down the middle of the island at an altitude of 500m (1,640ft), rising at the southern end to two granite peaks – the Donkey's Ears. The taller of these, Gunung Kajang, is 1,038m (3,405ft) high.

You can reach Tioman by flying from Kuala Lumpur (Sultan Abdul Aziz Airport) or by boat from the fishing village of Mersing. It takes about two hours to reach Tioman by express boat.

On the island's west coast, choose between luxury accommodation and the modest but comfortable guesthouses, chalets and simpler cabins on **Salang Beach** further north. Facilities around the main island port of **Tekek** include restaurants, diving shops and duty-free shops selling alcohol and cigarettes.

Most trips around the island are by boat, and the fishermen charge a reasonable fee. From Tekek, make the **forest trek** over the hill to the east coast. Take a dip at the hilltop waterfall, then make your way down to the beach at **Juara**, a village serving excellent seafood. Have another swim in the sea, and if you do not feel like trekking back, return to Tekek by boat.

Birdwatchers may see pied imperial pigeons, bulbuls, frigate birds, sunbirds and flowerpeckers. Characteristically for island forests, there are no large mammals. There have been some recent reptile discoveries.

THE SOUTH

The highway from Kuala Lumpur and Selangor leads through Negeri Sembilan, where the seaside resort town of Port Dickson is popular with day-trippers from Kuala Lumpur. Also on the west coast is the UNESCO World Heritage Site of Melaka (also known as Malacca); the rich tapestry of her history lies in the monuments and old homes, as well as the descendants of the colonisers – Malay, Indian, Chinese, Portuguese, Dutch and British. South of Melaka is Johor, where you can trek in a rainforest, catch some waves off the golden beaches of Desaru, sun-worship at any of Mersing's isles or visit the southernmost tip of mainland Asia at Tanjung Piai.

Negeri Sembilan
In the 'nine states' federated as one in the 18th century, you travel past vast palm oil and rubber plantations to the state capital of Seremban, 64km (40 miles) southwest of Kuala Lumpur. You can also take a train from KL to Gemas, where the 'Jungle Railway' line to the east coast begins.

On Pulau Tioman

Seremban

Here, the distinctive Minangkabau buffalo-horn roofs of Sumatran (Indonesian) heritage are evident, together with the more recent colonial Victorian style and the traditions of Chinese commercial shophouses. The main attractions are the **State Legislative Assembly Building**, a nest of nine roofs, one for each founding state; and the **State Museum Complex** on Jalan Sungai Ujung, where weapons as well as brass and silverware and a tableau portraying a grand royal wedding are on display. In the grounds opposite is the **Istana Ampang Tinggi**, a Malay prince's residence built entirely of wood. The neoclassical **State Library**, with its imposing colonial facade, was once the State Secretarial Building.

Sri Menanti

For what is probably the best original example of Minangkabau architecture, take a side trip to the old royal capital, 37km (23

Minangkabau architecture on the State Museum in
Negeri Sembilan

miles) east of Seremban on the Kuala Pilah Road. The ruler's
palace, **Istana Lama**, was the official residence of the state
royal family until 1931, replacing an earlier palace, which had
burnt down. The palace features 99 pillars, denoting 99 warriors of various *luak* (clans), and was built without nails. Inside,
you can see what it was like previously as a palace, including
the very steep stairs to the upper floors.

Port Dickson

About 34km (21 miles) from Seremban is the seaside town of
Port Dickson. The **Tanjung Tuan (Cape Rachado) Forest
Reserve** on the Melaka-Negeri Sembilan border is accessible
via the Jalan Pantai, 17km (11 miles) long, that passes beach-
side hotels, apartments and resorts. Beside forest trails, there
is a fine view of the Strait of Malacca from the lighthouse
believed to have been built by the Portuguese in the 16th

century to help guide ships into the Melakan port. The **Raptor Watch** festival every March coincides with thousands of birds of prey migrating from Sumatra back to their breeding grounds

in the northern hemisphere. About 26km (16 miles) north from here, just outside the town of Port Dickson, lies **Fort Lukut** (1847), built to protect the lucrative tin trade in the area. Inside is a foundation of an old palace and a royal burial ground. The fort is also known as Raja Jumaat, named after a 19th-century Bugis warrior.

Melaka

Easily reached by taxi or express bus from KL, **Melaka** (Malacca) ⓫ was built on the trading empires of spices and textiles and a history enveloped in the blood of battles as rival colonial powers challenged each other to take hold of the port. In its glorious 15th-century heyday, it was the most vital port in Southeast Asia, with as many as 2,000 ships docked here at any one time. Today, even as high-rises make their presence felt, the colonial past remains in the architecture and monuments. In 2008, UNESCO inscribed Melaka, together with George Town in Malaysia's northern state of Penang, as Historic Cities of the Strait of Malacca.

St Paul's Hill Civic Zone

The most prominent building overlooking the Dutch Square is the **Stadthuys** Ⓐ (Town Hall), dating from around 1650. It was originally the official residence of Dutch governors and their officers. Since 1980 the building has housed the History, Ethnography and Literature Museum, tracing the town's colonial and Malay past.

Christ Church, with an imposing red exterior, was built between 1741 and 1753, in commemoration of the centenary of the Dutch occupation, with later additions made by the British in the 19th century. Each of the long ceiling beams of the interior is hewn from one tree.

In the middle of the square is the **Queen Victoria Diamond Jubilee Fountain**, flanked by a mouse-deer statue. Behind the Stadthuys, a path leads to the remains of **St Paul's Church** ❸, built by a Portuguese captain, Duarte Coelho, as a chapel in 1521. Originally known as the Church of Our Lady of the Annunciation, it was renamed by the Dutch, who captured Melaka in 1641, and fell into disuse when Christ Church was built. In front of the church tower is a **statue of St Francis Xavier**, the Spanish Jesuit missionary who visited Melaka several times from 1545 until his death in 1553. In the church, a stone slab marks his tomb, empty since his remains were transported to Goa in India. Granite tombstones from the Dutch era stand against the walls. A Dutch and British **graveyard** is to be found further down the hill.

The **Porta de Santiago** ❹ (Santiago Gate) on Jalan Kota is all that remains of the 16th-century Portuguese fort, the **A' Famosa**. Sir Stamford Raffles, then a government secretary in Penang, saved it from total destruction. The date, 1670, and coat of arms were added to the gateway by the Dutch East India Company. Subsequent development of the area unearthed the foundations of the fortress. Nearby, at the edge of the shopping mall, is the foundation of the **Santiago Bastion**, one of the fortress' six original bastions during the Portuguese era. Next to it is the **mosaic-tiled pyramid** that commemorates Tunku Abdul Rahman's announcement in 1956 of Britain granting the country's independence. On 31 August 1957, he became the nation's first prime minister.

Back towards the river, along Jalan Kota, is the **Bastion of Courassa**, renamed Frederick Hendrik, and across Jalan

Melaka's Christ Church

Merdeka is the **Middleburg Bastion**, one of three additional bastions erected by the Dutch. The foundation is original but the bastion is a representation of what it may have looked like (its original height and size are unknown). Walk towards the river mouth to see the **Maritime Museum D**, housed in a model of the *Flor De La Mar*, a Portuguese ship laden with bullion and other valuables that sank off Melaka's coast. Exhibits include models of ships that have called at the port over its long history. Behind the ship, you can board the **Melaka River Cruise**, travelling past century-old townhouses and warehouses, and the gothic-style twin towers of the **Church of St Francis Xavier**.

Residential and Commercial Zone
This heritage zone is reached by crossing the bridge near the Stadthuys. The bridge was once the town's main strategic link between the port and city and the site of major battles against the European invaders.

In the grounds of A' Famosa fort

The living history of Melaka is to be found among the descendants of the original pioneers and entrepreneurs who married local Malay women. The Chinese-Malay descendants were called Baba (for the male) Nyonya (for the female). One of the Baba Nyonya families converted three houses on Jalan Tun Tan Cheng Lock (formerly Heeren Street) into the **Baba Nyonya Heritage Museum E** and a café with a guesthouse on the upper floors. Built in 1896 by rubber planter Chan Cheng Siew, the first two houses offer a vivid insight into the life and culture of the Baba Nyonya. In a style best described as Chinese Palladian, with its neoclassical columns and heavy hardwood doors, the furnishings and decor bear witness to the great prosperity of Baba entrepreneurs. The third house was originally the servants' quarters and far less ostentatious. At the top of the street at No. 8, is an 18th-century **Dutch-era shophouse** that has been authentically restored.

Melaka is a paradise for antiques hunters, filled with new and old Oriental treasures – porcelain, statues, jewellery, silverware and ornate 19th-century furniture. You will find a few **antique shops** on Jalan Hang Jebat (formerly Jonker Street). During the weekend, it becomes the **Jonker Street Weekend Night Market**, where you can satiate your appetite for local food.

Along Jalan Tokong and Jalan Tukang Emas, locally known as 'Harmony Street', are Chinese and Hindu temples and a Muslim mosque. The **Cheng Hoon Teng Temple** (Green Cloud Temple) **❻**, built in 1673, claims to be Malaysia's oldest Chinese temple. Dedicated to Kwan Yin, the Goddess of Mercy, it is flamboyantly decorated with multicoloured birds and flowers made from glass and porcelain. The bronze statue of Kwan Yin was brought back from India in the 19th century. The **Masjid Kampung Kling** on Jalan Tukang Emas (1748) has a multi-tiered roof with a Chinese-inspired minaret, while the nearby **Sri Poyyatha Vinayagar Moorthi Temple** (1781) is dedicated to the elephant god Ganesh, or Vinayagar.

The Peranakans

The Peranakan communities are descendants of early settlers who married the local women; their offspring were known as *peranakan*, Malay for 'locally born'. The most famous of the Peranakans are the Baba Nyonya community of Melaka (*baba*, male, *nyonya*, female). They demonstrate the Chinese genius for adapting to local circumstances without losing the essentials of their own culture. Their subtle blend of Chinese and Malay traditions – in cuisine, dress and language – began back in the 15th century, when the entourage of Princess Hang Li Po, daughter of the Emperor of China and betrothed to Mansur Shah of Melaka, intermarried with local gentry. Their numbers were boosted in subsequent centuries by the influx of merchants and entrepreneurs, largely from Fukien (Fujian) in southern China.

The Chitty or Peranakan Hindu are the offspring of Indian traders who first arrived in Melaka in the 1400s and chose to settle down as well. Even the Portuguese were smitten. 'I gave to each man his horse, a house and land,' wrote Afonso de Albuquerque in 1604, when he reported with pride to Portugal that 200 mixed marriages had taken place.

Nearby on Lorong Hang Jebat is the **Cheng Ho Cultural Museum**, which claims to be the site of one of the warehouses belonging to the Ming Dynasty's Admiral Zheng He (Cheng Ho). The warehouses were used to store treasures amassed from his travels between Melaka and Africa – he sailed back to China only when the winds were favourable.

The Chitty Village

Away from the old city centre, you may prefer to let a trishaw driver find the way to the nearby **Muzium Chetti**, next door to the **Chitty Village** on Jalan Gajah Berang. The one-room museum offers a historical overview of the Indian traders that first came to Melaka in the 1400s. They later married the local women, and, like the Baba Nyonya community, adopted certain cultural aspects of the Malays – in cuisine, dress and language.

The Portuguese Settlement

A short drive some 3km (2 miles) south of the town centre along Jalan Parameswara takes you to the heart of this little Eurasian community, peopled by descendants of the Portuguese colonists who married the local women. In the area around Jalan d'Albuquerque and **Medan Portugis** (Portuguese Square), you may hear snatches of Cristao, a 16th-century Portuguese dialect. The restaurants on and off the square serve good seafood. The community worships at the simple, unassuming **St Peter's Church**, 3km (2 miles) northwest from here on Jalan Bendahara, where Easter is an especially big event and attracts other ethnic groups to the great, candlelit procession.

Chinatown

Walk along Jalan Bunga Raya, the city's **Chinatown,** where you will see a variety of shops – selling anything from bales of cloth to rattan furniture and local delicacies. Off this street, between the former residence of a Chinese tycoon (now The

Antiques on Jonkers Street

Majestic Malacca hotel) and the Melaka River, lie the ruins of
Ermida do Rozário (Rosary Chapel). Prior to the completion
of St Peter's Church in 1710, Catholics would attend a service
here. It is also the final resting place of Emerici de Souza, a
Portuguese dignitary who died in 1842.

Bukit Cina
Inland, the hillside provides a Chinese cemetery for more than
12,500 graves, mostly horseshoe-shaped tombs. The **Poh San
Teng Temple** stands at the foot of Bukit Cina, honouring the
deity Tua Pek Kong. The temple was built so that offerings
could be made for the departed souls. Nearby is the **Perigi
Raja** (King's Well), dug in the 15th century.

Johor
Proximity to Singapore has buoyed the economy of Johor, the
peninsula's southernmost state, and that of its capital, Johor

A colourful trishaw driver

Bahru. Easy access from Singapore to east-coast resorts like Desaru and Sebana Cove in the southeast and the islands offshore from Mersing has also increased development of these destinations. In the 16th century, Johor provided refuge for the banished royal court of Melaka but today it offers many opportunities for tourism, from shopping to motor racing, horse riding to water sports, and adventure travel in the Endau-Rompin National Park. These relatively untouched forests at the border with Pahang delight ecotourists.

South of Melaka

The fishing port of **Muar** was of trading importance to the British in the 19th century, as can be seen in the graceful old neoclassical government offices. It was here that Australian troops made a heroic last stand against the Japanese advance on Singapore in January 1942. At **Ayer Hitam**, a wide range of Chinese-style pottery is on display beside the fruit market. The market town of **Batu Pahat** also offers respectable Chinese restaurants. The town witnessed a historic Melaka naval victory over the Siamese fleet in 1456.

The Endau-Rompin National Park

Straddling the Johor and Pahang border, **Endau-Rompin National Park**'s ⓬ 870 sq km (336 sq miles) of forest and

rivers is fast gaining a reputation among travellers as an
alternative to the more established Taman Negara. The
park is home to the Malayan
tiger, Asian elephant, wild
boar and the largest surviv-
ing population of Sumatran
rhinoceros in Peninsular
Malaysia. Other species
found here include the *bintu-*

Portuguese feasts

The Portuguese Eurasians
celebrate two feasts in June
– Festa San Juan (Feast of St
John the Baptist) and Festa
San Pedro (Feast of St Peter).
In the latter, fishing boats are
brightly decorated with sacred texts and neon lights to
honour the patron saint.

rong (bear cat) and the white-handed gibbon, the only ape species in the peninsula. Among the birdlife are drongos, many
species of hornbill and great argus pheasants. Endau-Rompin
is also home to the Orang Asli of the Jakun tribe.

Much less developed than the parks of Sarawak and Sabah
– and so far more pristine – Endau-Rompin offers a rare challenge to adventurous travellers. Facilities for accommodation
are limited to chalets, dormitories and three campsites in the
park, located at **Batu Hampar**, **Upeh Guling** and **Buaya
Sangkut**. You must employ a guide or go on a group tour.

From Johor Bahru, travel by the North–South Expressway to
Kluang, and take a detour to Kahang town. From there, only
a four-wheel-drive vehicle will take you along the 56km (35-
mile) jungle track to Kampung Peta, where there is a visitor
centre and point of entry to the national park. Otherwise, you
can get there via a three-hour boat journey from Felda Nitar
II. There is controlled entry and quite strident regulations gov-
erning park usage and duration periods.

Johor Bahru

Citizens of Singapore cross the causeway to Johor's state capital
to escape for the weekend and sample its lively nightlife at ZON
Johor Bahru, an integrated hotel, duty-free shopping and dining

Exploring the Endau-Rompin National Park

complex and ferry terminal (serving Indonesia's Batam and Bintan islands) on Jalan Ibrahim Sultan, or to head further north. Outside the restaurants and malls, travellers can visit the sprawling **market**, and nearby along the **Lido Waterfront** take a look at the gleaming white marble of the **Masjid Sultan Abu Bakar**, the **Royal Abu Bakar Museum** and the **Istana Gardens** of the old palace, with its Japanese teahouse and the sultan's private zoo, which is open to the public.

The neoclassical **Istana Besar** (palace) is now used for state ceremonies, the present-day sultans having moved further north to the modern **Istana Bukit Serene**, with its 32m (104ft) high tower. Other sights include the colonial-style clock tower overlooking the **Dataran Bandaraya** (City Square). The **Galeri Seni** is an art gallery, built in 1910 in a similar period style, exhibiting clothing, weapons, currency and manuscripts, as well as calligraphy, ceramic items and other artworks.

Johor's southern coastline

Johor has three RAMSAR protected wetlands of international importance. Unlike the Johor National Park at **Pulau Kukup** and **Tanjung Piai**, **Sungai Pulai** has no boardwalks to see the mangrove ecosystem, with its myriad wildlife such as smooth otters, dusky leaf monkeys, mudskippers and kingfishers. Sungai Pulai is close to the Malaysia–Singapore Second Link that bridges Johor with the western side of Singapore, and the best way to explore its mangroves is to join a **river cruise** led by the Orang Asli from the Orang Selatar tribe.

Desaru and the islands north

The 25km (15 miles) of golden sands of **Desaru** are accessible by road via Kota Tinggi or via the Senai–Desaru Highway from Senai International Airport. If you are travelling through **Kota Tinggi** and are an avid birdwatcher, it might be worthwhile booking in advance the permit to see the **Panti Bird Sanctuary,** about 8km (5 miles) north of Kota Tinggi. But if you are travelling via the Senai–Desaru Highway, make a detour to **Pasir Gudang**. The **Muzium Layang-Layang** here displays the story of kites and the annual World Kite Festival held early in the year is a colourful event not to be missed. For motor-racing enthusiasts, the **Johor Racing Circuit** offers spectators international motor-racing competitions.

Desaru is 55km (34 miles) further east and is the first major beach resort for Singaporeans. There are several premier resorts and golf courses here, but budget travellers will also find reasonable-value chalet accommodation.

Off the coast from the resorts of **Mersing**, there are several islands – **Pulau Rawa**, **Pulau Tengah**, **Pulau Besar**, **Pulau Tinggi** and **Pulau Sibu** – offering white sandy beaches, coral reefs and budget accommodation. Boats can be hired from Mersing to take you out to one of the more secluded islands.

EAST MALAYSIA

From rainforests to mountains, the states of Sarawak and Sabah offer enough adventure and natural beauty to make the journey across the South China Sea worthwhile. From shopping for exotic souvenirs and craftwork to dining in sea-side restaurants, to the thrill of riding in a longboat along river 'highways' deep in the forests, it is all there for the choosing. Music festivals in Sarawak, such as Rainforest World Music and Borneo Jazz, add a cultural dimension.

Historic evidence of the 'White Rajah' – the lineage that commenced with adventurer James Brooke in the mid-19th century and lasted until the start of World War II – can still be seen in Kuching, Sarawak's capital.

Away from the cities lie some natural treasures: Borneo's highest mountain (Gunung Kinabalu in Sabah), its longest river (the Rajang in Sarawak), its many caves (including the Niah and Mulu Caves in Sarawak), and natural parks with wonderful wildlife and flora. For a change of pace, there are plenty of beaches along the southern and eastern coasts and lots of islands for snorkelling or turtle-watching.

Getting around can be a challenge. The rivers, more numerous and much longer than on the peninsula, still provide the principal way into the interior, supplemented by smaller aircraft operated by Malaysia Airlines (MASwings).

Sarawak

It is just 90 minutes by air from Kuala Lumpur to Kuching, the historic capital of Malaysia's largest state – covering 124,967 sq km (48,250 sq miles). From the air you'll be able to see that Sarawak has the country's longest river, the Rajang, flowing 563km (350 miles) from the mountains on the Indonesian border to the South China Sea. The wealth of river systems among the forest terrain provides a vital link that will transport you to the tribes of the rainforest. Between taking river cruises or treks through the rainforest of Bako National Park, you can relax on the beaches of Santubong and Damai, just 40 minutes from Kuching. In eastern Sarawak, you can pursue more strenuous but exhilarating adventures in the Niah or Mulu cave systems.

Sarawak and Sabah operate their own immigration and visitors from peninsula are required to produce either their passports or identity cards.

Kuching

Unlike the other major towns of East Malaysia – Miri, Kota Kinabalu and Sandakan – Sarawak's state capital has preserved its colonial charm, having been spared the bombs of World War II. **Kuching** is built on a bend of the Sarawak River, 32km (20 miles) from the sea. The residence and fort built by the White Rajahs (see page 23) lie on the north bank, while on the southern bank is the greater part of the town, including Chinese and Indian merchants, major hotels and several colonial buildings, permanent vestiges of the past.

The colonial buildings include the **General Post Office**, noteworthy for its 1930s neoclassical design and pillars,

In an Annah Rais longhouse

Kuching's waterfront

and the **Court House**. The courthouse site was originally a German Lutheran mission before James Brooke, the first of the White Rajahs, turned it into a judicial administration office. In 1858 that building was demolished, making way for a second and later a third structure (the one that still stands), completed in 1874. State Council meetings continued to be held there until 1973. Today it houses the **Sarawak Tourism Complex**. The clock tower, whose bells still chime on the hour, was added in 1883. In front of the courthouse is the **Charles Brooke Memorial**, 6m (20ft) in height, which was built in 1924 in remembrance of the second White Rajah.

Along the **Kuching Waterfront**, north of the courthouse, is the **Square Tower**, which now houses souvenir shops.

West of the Courthouse is **Jalan India Mall**, a pedestrian mall marking the city's Muslim centre. Sarawak's oldest Indian mosque, **Masjid Bandar Kuching**, built in 1834, is here but there are plans to replace it with a three-storey mosque to accommodate the needs of the community. Still further west, the **Masjid Bahagian Kuching**, built in 1968 near the markets, is best seen from the other side of the river. A new mosque has also been built on the north side of the river.

Despite new high-rise constructions, the numerous traditional shophouses – both Chinese and Indian – ensure the city's heritage is still within reach. Chinese shophouses along **Jalan Padungan**, mostly built during the rubber boom of the 1920s and 1930s, offer a variety of restaurants, coffee houses and handicraft shops.

More colourful is the **Sunday Market** on Jalan Satok, which actually starts late on Saturday afternoon and extends through Sunday morning, offering a bewildering array of items; Dayaks come to sell fruit, vegetables and handicrafts and even more exotic items from the forest. Clothes and

Aborigines of Northern Borneo

These many tribes were once collectively known as Land or Sea Dayaks.
Iban, the largest indigenous group in Sarawak, dwell in longhouses along lowland river banks. They farm rice, rubber and pepper.
Melanau inhabit the coastal plain east of Kuching, where they fish and grow cassava.
Bidayuh, the original Land Dayaks who allied with the White Rajahs of the 19th century, are longhouse dwellers of western Sarawak.
Kenyah and Kayan are two distinct tribes but often live side by side along the upper reaches of Sarawak's Baram and Rajang rivers. They farm hill rice and rubber, and rear pigs and poultry.
Penan, the last of East Malaysia's nomads, stay upriver well clear of civilisation. The men make superb weapons – machetes and blowpipes – and the women are renowned as basket-weavers.
Kadazan/Dusun, Sabah's biggest tribe, have adapted smoothly to urban life – and Christianity – in Kota Kinabalu. Others live on terraced hills around Gunung Kinabalu.
Bajau are Muslim seafarers affectionately known as 'Sea Gypsies'. Their landlubber cousins are admired as daring cowboy cattle-breeders.
Murut are hunters in the hill country along the Sabah–Sarawak border.

Dragon wall carving at Kuek Seng Onn Temple

household goods appeal to the locals.

East of the courthouse, the **Tua Pek Kong Temple** and the **Chinese History Museum** are near a group of five-star hotels that line the river. The temple, also known as the Siew San Teng Temple, was built in 1876 and is the oldest in Kuching; it remains an active place of worship. The nearby museum traces the long history of the Chinese in Sarawak, who lived there well before the arrival of James Brooke. Another temple is the **Kuek Seng Ong Temple**, on Lebuh Wayang, built in 1895. For a small fee, venture across the Sarawak River by *tambang* (ferry) to view the **Astana** (1870) and recently renovated **Fort Margherita** (1879). The Astana (which means 'palace' in Malay) was originally the Brooke family's home. It comprises three bungalows under a single roof and is built off the ground, supported by brick pillars. The building has a library and a collection of artefacts associated with the Brooke family. The ground floor was the location for many garden parties hosted by the Rajahs; it was also used as an internment centre for Japanese prisoners of war in World War II. It is now the residence of the Governor of Kuching, the Yang Di-Pertua Negeri. Set among beautiful grounds, it is, unfortunately, not open to the public.

Up the hill to the right from the Astana, the road leads to Fort Margherita, which used to house the Muzium Polis. The white-turreted edifice was built by Sir Charles Brooke along the lines of an English medieval castle and named after his wife, Margaret. It was converted to a police museum in 1971, but this was closed in 2004. The views from here across the river to the city are most pleasant and the journey across the river on a small and colourful *tambang* has to be one of the last great river crossings in the whole of Southeast Asia. The boats depart from along the waterfront.

On the south side of the river, another colonial building is the **Round Tower** on Jalan Tun Abang Haji Openg. It was originally designed as a dispensary when built in the 1880s.

Also south of the river on Jalan Tun Abang Haji Openg is the **Sarawak Museum**, which has one of the best collections of folk art and flora and fauna in Southeast Asia. The museum is divided between the old and new wings, connected by a footbridge across the road. The former was built in 1891 and styled along the lines of a Normandy townhouse; it is devoted to Sarawak's rich history and diverse cultures. Another wing, completed in 1983, has more galleries and archaeological exhibits, including a reconstruction of early human settlements at the Niah Caves. There is a book and souvenir shop.

Within the museum's grounds are the **Botanical Gardens** and the **Heroes Memorial**, the latter commemorating the dead from World War II, the Communist Emergency and the Confrontation with Indonesia. Adjacent to the new wing

Kuching, Sarawak's capital

In Malay, *kuching* means 'cat', but no one knows for sure why Sarawak's capital has this name. One theory is that it was named after the stray cat population that was rife at the time of James Brooke's arrival, although locals argue the town was named after the tidal stream that originated from Bukit Mata Kuching, where many *mata kuching* (cat eye) fruit trees grow. The most plausible theory? Brooke had named the Sarawak River port 'Cochin', after the one in India. If mispronounced, it sounds like *kuching*.

of the Sarawak Museum is the **Muzium Islam Sarawak** (Sarawak Islamic Museum), with its seven galleries.

Highlights of the old wing include a reconstructed **Iban Longhouse**, complete with totem pole, hornbill-feather headdresses and skulls of head-hunting victims; the **Kenyah Tree of Life Mural**, repainted from one at a longhouse at Long Nawang; **Melanau dolls**, which serve as charms against disease and to lure animals to traps; and specimens of Alfred Russel Wallace's extensive collection of insects.

The new wing is home to galleries of **Hindu and Buddhist sculptures**; Chinese, Thai, Japanese and European **ceramics** and **brassware**; a model of the **Niah Caves** (see page 112), with their birds, bats and other fauna; **Stone Age artefacts**; and **funeral boats** from the 8th century AD. A photographic history of Kuching is also interesting.

One gallery has become the world's first **Cat Museum**, in honour of the city's feline mascot (see page 107).

Around Kuching

The fishing village and peninsula of **Santubong** is 40 minutes from Kuching. There you will find beach resorts and cultural sights, plus trails for forest trekking, bike riding and golf. **Gunung Santubong** (810m/ 2,655ft) peers down on **Damai**, where you will find beach resorts. Nearby is the **Sarawak Cultural Village**, 7 hectares (17 acres) of craft demonstrations and cultural performances. Described as a 'living museum', it provides an opportunity to learn about Sarawak's rich culture.

In the Sarawak Museum

In July each year the village comes alive with the Rainforest World Music Festival, a celebration of music and friendship.

There are three beach resorts and a rainforest resort at Damai, each offering a range of water sports, jungle trekking trips and cultural activities. Two of the resorts, both located at **Teluk Penyu Beach**, are within easy reach of the Cultural Village. Outside the village, there is access to local longhouses as well as trips to the Bako National Park, local fishing villages and nearby islands, and river cruises to spot dolphins, proboscis monkeys and migratory water birds around **Bako-Buntal Bay**.

In Sarawak two major centres are involved with orang-utan rehabilitation. **Semenggoh Wildlife Centre**, southwest of Kuching, rehabilitates orphaned babies and adults who have been kept as domestic pets. At **Matang Wildlife Centre**, northwest of Kuching, the focus of their work is on the orang-utans, but there are also enclosures for sambar deer, crocodiles, sun bears, civets and bear cats, as well as aviaries holding hornbills, sea eagles and other birdlife from Sarawak.

You can visit old gold mines in **Bau**, the historic gold-mining town about 36km (22 miles) south of Kuching. Although

Alfred Russel Wallace, Nature Sleuth

A contemporary of Charles Darwin, Alfred Russel Wallace proved a true detective in his pioneering research in evolution theory and 'biogeography' – the geographical distribution of animals and plants. In Malaysia, he is best known as the 'discoverer' of the national butterfly, the green-and-black 'Rajah Brooke Birdwing'. But his most intriguing contributions came in the field of natural mimicry. Beyond the familiar camouflage techniques of chameleons and stick insects, he watched viceroy butterflies trick birds by cultivating a resemblance to the monarch butterfly, which the birds hate. He also discovered ant-eating spiders that look like their prey.

A dance performance in traditional dress at the Sarawak Cultural Village

mining activities in the area ceased in 1921, illegal diggers continue to mine occasionally. Nearby, the **Wind and Fairy Caves** are two show caves worth a visit.

Bako National Park

Both **Bako National Park** ⓭ and **Kubah National Park** are within easy reach of Kuching. Sarawak's oldest national park, Bako is also one of the smallest, covering just 27 sq km (10 sq miles), but it offers great opportunities to see a wide range of animal and plant life. Since the park is located just one hour (37km/23 miles) from Kuching, visitors have a choice between a day trip or an overnight stay; accommodation includes dormitories and chalets. You must first travel to Kampung Bako, where you can get a boat to transport you to the park headquarters at Telok Assam. The paunchy **proboscis monkey**, with its long nose, is the major attraction, but you can also see silver-leaf monkeys and long-tail macaques, as well as mouse deer, monitor lizards and a variety of birdlife.

At Bako there are 16 well-marked, colour-coded jungle trails with bridges over the swamps to the best spots for viewing flora and wildlife. Twelve of the trails lead off from the right of the park's headquarters, just across from the arrival jetty. The **Tanjong Sapi Trail**, a 30-minute steep climb up to the cliff-tops overlooking the bay that fronts the park headquarters, is recommended.

On the **Lintang Trail**, a small observation hide at the Lintang Salt Lick offers the chance to see the animals at close quarters as they drink. Besides its good hilltop view over the forest, the **Bukit Tambi Trail** is home to several specimens of carnivorous plants: the bladderwort, pitcher plant and sundew (Venus flytrap).

Telok Delima and **Telok Paku trails** are the best paths for viewing the proboscis monkeys as they like to bed down in trees near the seashore. Very often, they will have been watching you long before you spot them, and if your presence upsets them, they will just honk and disappear. Along the seashore, keep a look out for hairy-nosed otters.

Visiting a Longhouse

The opportunity to see the tribes of Sarawak in their forest homes is a privilege not to be missed. However, tours to some longhouses have acquired the artificial character of a 'tribal theme park'. As tourism grows and the popularity of such expeditions increases, it is a trend difficult to escape, the only real alternative being to travel even further into the forests at added expense. But the adoption by some villagers of Western clothing or items like televisions and radios shouldn't put you off.

On offer for adventurous travellers is a choice between a day trip, an overnight stay at a guesthouse near a longhouse, or a stay in a longhouse itself. Tours from Kuching usually start very early and involve a two- to five-hour road journey to the river and then a one-hour cruise by longboat. Tour operators usually have exclusive arrangements with particular longhouses.

The format of a visit varies, but it may include cultural performances soon after arrival for day-trippers or at the day's end as evening entertainment for those staying longer. The standard tour is an initial orientation to the longhouse, highlighting the *bilik* (apartments), as distinct from the *ruai* (communal areas). Tour groups are often greeted with *tuak*, a sweet wine made from glutinous rice, and a welcome dance. The musical and cultural performance includes a traditional dance. Demonstrations of the blowpipe and cockfighting are also likely to be on the agenda.

Before you leave, your tour guide will remind you to make sure that you have gifts – preferably nutritious food, clothes or children's books – which you can buy during one of the bus stopovers on the way. Sweets and junk food are inappropriate. Malaysian tourism authorities are also able to offer advice on reputable tour operators in Kuching who organise visits on a small scale so as not to offend tribal customs.

Tours are available to Iban longhouses around Kuching, and Bidayuh longhouses in the hill regions. Visits to Iban communities are possible along the **Skrang** and **Batang Ai** rivers. To the east of Kuching you can visit the Kenyah and Kayan tribes. Excursions are organised either via Miri from Kuala Baram along the majestic **Baram River**, or via Sibu, from Kapit or Belaga, up the **Rajang River**. The Rajang is considered Malaysia's greatest river at some 560km (350 miles) long; a journey along it is one of the world's last great travel adventures. The approach to Belaga entails a passage through the Rajang's **Pelagus Rapids**. There are seven in all: Bidai (big mat), Nabau (python), Lunggak (dagger), Pantu (sago), Sukat (measure), Mawang (fruit) and, most ominously, Rapoh (tomb).

Niah National Park

At **Niah Caves** ⓮ visitors can see the earliest traces of Homo sapiens in Sarawak; they lived in the area up to 40,000 years ago. Later the caves were used as burial grounds, and they are now the hunting ground of collectors of birds' nests located on the cave roofs. The caves and surrounding 3,149-hectare

Stripping canes for basket weaving in an Annah Rais longhouse

(7,775-acre) park are 480km (300 miles) up the coast from Kuching, hidden within the forests around Miri.

Adventurer A. Hart Everett came across the caves in the 1870s, but it was not until 1958 that local explorer and Sarawak Museum curator Tom Harrison made the important discovery of a human skull dating back some 40,000 years, together with 1,200-year-old red hematite rock paintings. The fragments of the Deep Skull (so-called because it was found deep within an ancient pile of bat guano), together with tools, earthenware pots, jars and later bronze jewellery found nearby, are on display in the Sarawak Museum.

The park, near the town of Batu Niah, is midway between **Bintulu** and **Miri**, the latter a boom city known for its oil exploration. The caves are accessible by road from either settlement, taking at least two hours from Miri and three hours from Bintulu. The park's headquarters is at **Pengkalan Batu**, and you will need to obtain a permit either here or in Miri.

From here, you cross the Sungei Niah (or Niah River) by sampan, then follow the 3km (2-mile) boardwalk to the caves. For the cave tour, be sure to take a powerful flashlight, sturdy walking shoes with a good grip and a change of clothes – the heat and humidity are quite intense.

First seen is the **Trader's Cave**, so-called because of its role as a meeting place for bird's-nest gatherers and merchants. The main or **Great Cave** is a hollow 400m (1,312ft) up in the sandstone Subis Plateau. Besides giant crickets and scorpions (from which the extension of the boardwalk through the cave keeps you safe), the cave is home to millions of bats and swiftlets. The Deep Skull and other relics were discovered here.

Life in the longhouse

A typical longhouse is a communal dwelling of perhaps 20 'apartments', attached one to the other and extended as each family adds a unit of parents with children. Erected close to the river, it is built of sturdy, axe-hewn timber, preferably Sarawak's coveted *belian* ironwood. The structure is raised above the ground on massive pillars – a technique evolved in the past to resist enemy attacks rather than mere river flooding.

A notched tree trunk serves as a stairway to the outer, open veranda, where the families congregate, dry their washing or lay out their fish, spices, fruit, nuts and vegetables. On the inner, closed veranda are the communal 'lounges', kept for recreation and ceremonies.

Off to the side behind partitions, family dwellings consist of bedrooms and kitchens. An attic under the roof is used for storing grain or rice. The attic sometimes doubles as a weaving room.

Modern times have brought running tap water, electricity generators, cooking stoves, radio and television. However, people also keep their traditions, wearing sarongs and proudly bearing hornbill tattoos on their throat and arms. Hanging from pillars and rafters are the ancestral head-hunting trophies – believed to give the clan strength and good fortune.

Niah Cave

The bats' daily droppings furnish one tonne of highly valued guano fertiliser. But more lucrative than the guano are the swiftlets' edible nests – used to make bird's-nest soup – for which Chinese merchants are prepared to pay hundreds of dollars per kilo (about 100 nests), reselling them for thousands. Park authorities are increasingly concerned about the impact of the ongoing harvest on the swiftlets' survival. The rush of nesting swiftlets flying into the cave at the day's end, while nocturnal bats rush past into the evening sky, is a spectacular sight.

The boardwalk continues through the Great Cave down to the **Painted Cave**, also accessible without a guide. Discovered in 1958 along with the Deep Skull, its wall paintings representing red stick-figures of spreadeagle dancers were executed in a mixture of betel juice and lime around AD700. This cave was probably also used as a burial chamber.

Nearby are several forest trails, with the **Bukit Kasut** and the **Madu trails** both clearly marked. Look out for long-tailed

The underground caves in Gunung Mulu National Park

macaques, together with a range of birdlife such as bulbuls, tailor birds, crested wood partridges, trogons and hornbills.

Gunung Mulu National Park

Among the largest limestone cave systems in the world, the UNESCO World Heritage Site of **Gunung Mulu National Park ⑮** (53,000 hectares/130,600 acres) is one of Sarawak's most important attractions. The cave system of 150km (94 miles) was first explored between 1976 and 1984 and requires a minimum two-day/one-night stay to be fully appreciated. The trip is demanding, and you need to be in good shape, especially if you are looking to undertake the climb to the limestone-sculpted pinnacles on Gunung Api (Fire Mountain).

A 35-minute flight from Miri arrives at the airport near the park's headquarters. The alternative (by land and boat) also starts from Miri and is a four-stage trip. First, you travel by bus or taxi to Kuala Baram, at the mouth of the Batang Baram.

From here, you take an express boat to **Marudi**, before meeting up with the noon boat to **Long Terawan**, followed by a third longboat along the Sungei Tutoh and Sungei Melinau to the park's headquarters. This is the only alternative to the air trip and requires almost a full day of travel by bus and boat. The flight from Miri over rainforest in a small aircraft is considered the best way to begin your stay at Mulu and is also recommended for the return journey.

There are four main 'show caves' at Mulu – Deer, Lang's, Clearwater and Wind – as well as countless other 'wild caves', which are either too dangerous or too ecologically fragile to visit without special permits and qualified guides.

To give you an idea of the vast scale of the caverns, **Sarawak Chamber**, reputed to be the largest cave in the world, is said to be capable of holding 40 jumbo jets. Tours began in 1998, but entry is usually restricted to seasoned cavers. If you wish to see this spectacular chamber, ask for details well in advance when making your booking.

Bird's-nest soup

Descendants of the nomadic Penan people who rediscovered the Niah Caves' bird's-nest riches in the 19th century divide up the cave into jealously guarded 'stakes', handed down from father to son. To scrape the nests from the cave ceiling, the Penan climb more than 60m (200ft) up a series of swaying bamboo poles tied together, or through narrow 'chimneys' inside the rock. As the old song says, 'A lotta men did and a lotta men died' – nobody knows how many.

White-bellied swiftlets are responsible for the high-priced nests, made from pure saliva rendered particularly glutinous by a diet of algae. An inferior product is furnished by 'black-nest' swiftlets, who mix feathers in with the saliva. While not for everyone, Chinese diners insist that the viscous, translucent soup is delicious.

The Pinnacles

Nearest to the park's headquarters are the **Deer Cave** and Lang's Cave. The Deer Cave, with an enormous entrance and a passage 2km (1 mile) long and up to 220m (720ft) high, was once a shelter for deer. It is uncertain whether it was also used as a human burial ground, as other caves in the system were. Like many other large, open caves, it is home to millions of bats, which fly out in a cloud at dusk in search of food. Noteworthy is 'Adam and Eve's shower', a cascade of water falling 120m (393ft) from the cave's ceiling. Deep within the cave – reached after about an hour's walking – is a hidden green valley known as the **Garden of Eden**.

Lang's Cave, nearby, was discovered by a Berawan man called Lang who was out hunting wild boar and, although smaller, it has a variety of stalactites and stalagmites and spectacular rock curtains.

Both the **Clearwater** and **Wind Caves** are reached by longboat from park headquarters. The Clearwater Cave's passage extends for 50km (31 miles). After passing the moss-covered stalactites near the entrance, you'll need a good flashlight in order to see the limestone formations. Wind Cave is accessible to hardy cavers from near the Clearwater Cave, but other visitors must make their entry from the riverbank.

Exploring the **Pinnacles**, 900m (2,950ft) up the side of Gunung Api, will add extra days to the tour, but there are few sights to match these

Mulu's caves

With permits, experienced cavers can explore Mulu's less accessible caves and wade chest-deep through underground streams. The best guides will provide miner's helmets with built-in lamps to explore the pitch-black caves. Your own equipment should include very strong shoes made of rubber rather than leather, lots of socks, tough old clothes, a pair of gloves and a light sleeping bag.

gigantic stone needles thrusting like petrified hooded ghosts above the dark-green canopy of the forest. Extra time, too, is required if you wish to attempt the climb up **Gunung Mulu** (2,376m/7,793ft), whose summit was successfully reached by Lord Shackleton in 1932 after earlier known attempts in the 19th century had failed. The ascent of Gunung Mulu alone can take up to five days, although experienced climbers have made the journey in less than two.

The richness of the park's flora and fauna has been the topic of many scientific studies, revealing 1,500 species of flowering plant, 4,000 varieties of fungus, 75 species of mammal, 262 species of bird, 50 species of reptile and 281 species of butterfly. Birdlife includes stork-billed kingfishers along rivers and strawheaded bulbuls in the forests.

To observe wildlife in the forest canopy, you can use either the 30m (98ft) tall **tower and bird hide** near the park headquarters or the slightly lower **Mulu Canopy Skywalk** that is 480m (1,574ft) long.

Sabah

Covering the northern tip of Borneo, Sabah lies just clear of the cyclones that regularly sweep down across the Philippines, and so has been dubbed by generations of sailors the 'Land Below the Winds'. Its capital, Kota Kinabalu – popularly known as KK – looks over the South China Sea, with the Sulu Sea to the northeast and the Celebes Sea to the south.

KK lies in the shadow of the Crocker Mountain Range, home of Gunung Kinabalu, one of Southeast Asia's tallest mountains at 4,095m (13,435ft). The Kinabalu National Park is just one of several protected regions in the state.

Beadwork for sale at the Kota Kinabalu Handicraft Market

The capital also serves as a gateway for visits to an offshore national park of coral islands. On the east coast, Sandakan provides a base for visiting the Turtle Islands Marine Park, the famous orang-utans of Sepilok and the Kinabatangan River. Visitors can choose from fishing, snorkelling, deep-sea diving, leisurely coral cruises in the beautiful waters surrounding Sabah, or just exploring KK's markets.

Kota Kinabalu

Known as Jesselton (after Sir Charles Jessel, chairman of the North Borneo Chartered Co.) until World War II, **Kota**

Kinabalu was renamed Api (Fire) by the occupying Japanese. Today's KK was rebuilt from the ashes of the war after Allied bombing razed the city during the Japanese occupation. KK is at present a prosperous and busy sea port, with a growing manufacturing base and a population of more than 450,000. Rebuilt in a modern style, it is blessed with a beautiful natural setting: tree-clad coral islands off the coast and the dramatic backdrop of Gunung Kinabalu to the west. The city is generally used as a base for visiting the surrounding national parks. You'll find a **tourist information office** (a former post office) on Jalan Gaya.

The **Masjid Bandaraya** (City Mosque) in Teluk Likas, about 3km (2 miles) north of KK, shares similar features with the Nabawi Mosque in Medina. South of KK is the **Sabah State Museum and Heritage Village** on Jalan Bukit Istana Lama. The museum is styled along the lines of Murut and Rungus longhouses, and is set in grounds where you will also find a number of steam engines. Its historic photographic collection provides a chance to see the township as it was before the devastation of war.

Next door is the **Science and Technology Centre** and an **Art Gallery**. Across from the museum is an **Ethnobotanic Garden**, offering the chance to see a range of tropical plants.

One block east of Jalan Gaya is the **Atkinson Clock Tower**, built in 1905. Along with the tourist information office, it is one of the few pre-war structures still standing.

Walk up the hill to enjoy the view from the **Signal Hill Observatory**. One of the most popular markets in town is the **Jalan Gaya Street Fair**, held every Sunday morning. The **Handicraft Market** is at the waterfront, near the general and fish markets.

On the north side of town is the gleaming **Sabah Foundation** building, a 30-storey landmark. Construction of the tower was financed by timber royalties to the state, after the Sabah Foundation, devoted to state educational projects, was established in 1966. Views from the revolving restaurant and bar, on the 18th floor, are stunning. Plan to be here at sunset to appreciate the best views of KK.

The Coral Islands

Just a brief boat ride from KK are the five islands of the **Tunku Abdul Rahman Park**, which was created in 1974. Take the boat transfers from the Jesselton Point Ferry Terminal located at the end of Lorong Satu for either a group or individual tour to the islands. All five islands lie within an 8km (5-mile) radius and provide first-class beaches and superb opportunities for swimming and snorkelling, and there are boardwalk trails into the islands' forested interiors.

Looking over Kinabalu Park's mountains and rainforest

Pulau Gaya is the largest of the coral islands. The park headquarters here can give you information about the flora and fauna, both underwater and in the forest. The sandy **Police Beach** on the north shore is good for swimming and exploring marine life among the coral reefs. On the boardwalk trail across a mangrove-swamp forest, look out for monkeys, bearded pigs and pied hornbills.

Some of the best nature trails are on neighbouring **Pulau Sapi**, a 10-hectare (25-acre) islet off the northwestern coast of Pulau Gaya. South of Sapi is **Pulau Manukan**, the most developed of the islands, with hilltop and beach-side chalets, a restaurant, swimming pool, and tennis and squash courts. Tiny **Pulau Mamutik**, covering just 6 hectares (15 acres) and largely unspoiled, with plenty of reefs at its northeastern end, is very popular with divers and snorkellers. The most remote and least developed island, with the park's finest coral reefs and abundant marine life, **Pulau Sulug** offers a more tranquil and deserted atmosphere.

Around Kota Kinabalu

From the bus terminal near Jalan Undan, 10km (6.2 miles) east of KK, inexpensive journeys can be made to locations not far from the city. Visit one of the many *tamu* (village markets) held on different days of the week – ask at Kota Kinabalu's tourist information office. The best are at **Tuaran**, 33km (20 miles) from KK, and further north at Kota Belud, where you will find the **Mengkabong** and **Penambawan** Bajau villages.

At Donggongon in the village of Kuai, 10km (6 miles) south of KK on Penampang River, is the Kampung Monsopiad. It was built to commemorate the legendary warrior Monsopiad, whose forte was beheading his enemies. Forty-two of his 'trophies' are on show at the **Monsopiad Cultural Village**.

To view the nearby tropical forests, ride on the railway to **Beaufort**, and another 40km (25 miles) northwest to the town of **Tenom**, with its **Agricultural Research Station**. Nearby, tour operators out of KK run **rafting trips** on the raging Padas River. Although the new North Borneo Railway train begins its journey at Tanjung Aru, you can save time by taking a taxi to Beaufort and then another from Tenom back to Kota Kinabalu. At Beaufort, Chinese shophouses stand on stilts next to the Padas River. The **North Borneo Railway**, an old-fashioned steam locomotive, runs to Papar a few times a week.

South from KK, heading towards the Crocker Mountain Range, is the **Rafflesia Information Centre**. This is dedicated

A Kadazan dancer at Monsopiad Cultural Village

to the world's largest flower, the rafflesia, of which there are 14 varieties. About 300km (186 miles) northwest of KK and reached by a 75-minute flight is the diving and migratory birdwatching haven of Pulau Layang Layang (open March–July), where divers can see, among other large pelagic creatures, schools of hammerhead sharks and manta rays.

Kinabalu Park

The refreshing temperatures and spectacular scenery make a journey to **Kinabalu Park ⑯**, a UNESCO World Heritage Site, more than worthwhile. Even if you avoid the vigorous climb to the mountain's summit, the scenery, plants and wildlife close to the park's headquarters are rewarding. Looming huge and dark in the light of dawn, the peak is revealed in its full splendour, but morning clouds often sweep upwards again to shroud it in mist. At 4,095m (13,435ft), **Gunung Kinabalu** is one of the highest peaks between the Himalayas and New Guinea. Its name means 'sacred home of the dead' to the Kadazan who live on its lower slopes. The park can be reached by road 90km (56 miles) from Kota Kinubalu. There is a special bus service from KK, but arrive early, as it departs once full. The trip to the park headquarters takes at least two hours, though only one and a half hours on return. There are also regular buses plying the highway between KK and Sandakan. The journey from Kota Kinabalu to the park and the climb up into the Crocker Range takes you through Malaysia's varieties of forest and landscape, from lowland dipterocarp forest to subalpine meadow.

The park covers 754 sq km (291 sq miles), with temperatures far cooler than on the coast. They ease to a gentle 20°C (68°F) at park headquarters and can drop to freezing point at the resthouse where climbers spend the night prior to their assault on the summit, so warm clothing is a must, as well as rainproof clothing for those climbing the mountain.

To climb the summit, book at the **Sabah Parks Headquarters** in Kota Kinabalu well in advance, especially in April, July, August and December. The climb takes two days, with an overnight stay halfway up. Foreigners pay more than locals. The park has a good restaurant and accommodation ranging from chalets to simple hostels. At the park's headquarters arrangements are made for mountain guides, porters and transport to the station where the climb begins. Instead of heading for the summit, you could book with **Mountain Torq** and traverse the world's highest via ferrata or "iron road" on the northern face of the mountain. Hardy souls may like to swim in the cool Liwagu River nearby. A small **Mountain Garden** provides a good introduction to the plant life you will find in Kinabalu's forest.

The pride of the mountain's plant life is its 1,200 different orchids, found up to an altitude of 3,800m (12,464ft). Ferns are also present in their hundreds. Rhododendron-lovers may find 25 different varieties, together with 60 types of oak and chestnuts. But the most fascinating flora remains the pink-speckled, carnivorous pitcher plants.

Many of the local forest's 100 mammals are difficult to spot; the few orang-utans, for instance, are practically invisible, but you can at least hear the gibbons whooping. Besides the usual sambar and mouse deer, bearded pigs and clouded leopards, there are 28 species of squirrel, as well as the slow loris and the western tarsier. Kinabalu also has some 326 species of birds, including the scarlet sunbird, whitehead's spider-hunter, grey drongo, crested serpent eagle and white-rumped shama.

Meals and bedding are provided at the mountain lodges for the overnight stop. Rates differ between weekdays and weekends. Armed with warm and rainproof clothing, flashlight, and bananas and chocolate for energy, you make an early-morning start. After a stretch of road, the climb proper begins at **Timpohon Gate**. As you climb, you will notice the change from bamboo groves to oaks (the forest here has 40 different varieties), myrtle, laurel and moss-covered pines. The trees become more gnarled and stunted as you approach the barren granite plateau at the summit.

The first shelter at **Carson's Falls** is at 1,951m (6,400ft). The best chance to see pitcher plants on the trail is at the **Second Shelter** on the trail at 2,134m (7,000ft), but remember, no picking. You make your overnight stop at the **Laban Rata Resthouse** or the **Panar Laban Hut**, **Waras Hut** or **Gunting Lagadan** at 3,353m (11,000ft). Panar Laban means

The pitcher plant

The pitcher plant consists of a bowl often shaped like a miniature tuba with a curved lid sticking upright when open. Why do insects fall in? Those that go for the nectar under the pitcher lid get away safely. Others going for the nectar glands under the pitcher's rim fall into a digestive liquid mixture of rainwater and enzymes. Unable to climb back up the sticky, scaly interior, they drown and are slowly digested. Cashing in on the activity around these plants, some spiders spin webs across the inside of the pitcher's mouth and catch the falling insects.

The giant of the species is the *Nepenthes rajah*, with one pitcher measuring a record 46cm (18in) and holding 4 litres (7 pints) of water. They have been found digesting frogs and even rats.

Gunung Kinabalu and its foothills

Place of Sacrifice: here seven white chickens and seven eggs are offered each year by Kadazan climbers to the spirits of the sacred mountain.

To get to the summit at sunrise, you must get up at about 2am and make your way up across a barren granite plateau. The **Sayat-Sayat Hut**, 3,811m (12,500ft), is the last shelter before the summit. Directly to the north are the **Donkey's Ears** rocks, and behind them the **Ugly Sister Peak**, as you make your way west to **Low's Peak** (4,095m/13,435ft), the highest of the mountain's nine peaks. The view from the Crocker Range and towards the Philippines is staggering. But you cannot stay long, as the summit soon becomes enveloped in mid-morning mists, making the descent treacherous for even experienced climbers.

Poring Hot Springs

The **Poring Hot Springs**, 37km (23 miles) from the park headquarters, offer great relief after the tough climb down the mountain. The springs, with their soothing sulphur baths, were developed by the Japanese during World War II. Cool off at the **Langanan Waterfall** along one of the trails, or at the **Kepungit Waterfall**, a site rich in butterflies and bat-filled caves. Nearby are groves of bamboo (poring means bamboo in Kadazan), a canopy walk, lodgings in chalets and hostels and a campsite.

Sandakan

Stretched along a narrow strip of land between steep hills and the Sulu Sea, **Sandakan** is the gateway to the Turtle Islands Marine Park, the Gomantong Caves, the Sepilok Orang-Utan Rehabilitation Centre and the Labuk Bay Proboscis Monkey Sanctuary. Once the capital of British North Borneo, modern Sandakan, like Kota Kinabalu, was devastated during World War II, leaving little evidence of the former township.

The lively **Central Market** at the waterfront is a good starting point for visitors. Sandakan's oldest temple, built in the 1880s, is dedicated to the **Goddess of Mercy**, although modernisation has detracted from its character. The ornate **Puu Jih Shih Buddhist Temple**, ablaze with dragons and gilded Buddhas, stands on the hilltop above Tanah Merah, south of Sandakan town.

You can also tour the home of **Agnes Keith**, an American writer whose life in Sandakan from 1932–54, including experiences in a prisoner-of-war camp, was documented in three novels, including *Land Below the Wind*. Her prewar home was destroyed but reconstructed and is now a museum. Next door is the superb English Teahouse and Restaurant.

Other links to the war include the **Sandakan Memorial Park** on the site of the former prisoner-of-war camp in Taman Rimba, off Labuk Road. It commemorates the Allied soldiers who died during the Japanese occupation and serves as a remembrance of the Death March by 2,400 mostly Australian soldiers – of whom just six survived – from the camp to Ranau in September 1944.

There is also a small Japanese graveyard in the corner of the old cemetery on the hills overlooking the town.

The Lower Kinabatangan River Basin

The **Kinabatangan Basin**, 80km (50 miles) southwest of Sandakan, offers a good chance to catch sight of a range of wildlife, especially Borneo's pygmy elephants, hornbills, monitor lizards, macaques and orang-utans, not to mention the elusive proboscis monkey. The Kinabatangan is a rewarding river for wildlife fans, with trips organised by Sandakan tour operators.

At Poring Hot Springs

The Sepilok Orang-Utan Rehabilitation Centre

A 30-minute drive west of Sandakan, the **Sepilok Orang-Utan Rehabilitation Centre ⑰** is a nature reserve that provides rehabilitation and care for young orang-utans, previously held in captivity. This prepares them to live alone in the forest. Boardwalk trails take visitors to the feeding areas.

These highly theatrical apes exist at three levels here: tame, entirely in the care of zoologists; semi-tame, living within reach of the sanctuary's feeding points; and wild, having moved off to remote parts of the forest away from their prying human cousins. Many of the orang-utans are as curious as the visitors. They have flashy tastes, preferring to snatch at bright objects rather than dull ones. They also have a good

Malaysia's famous inhabitant,
the orang-utan

sense of parody. Watching someone put up an umbrella in the rain, they will immediately mimic this, using leaves and twigs.

Optimistic figures put the number of orang-utans at around 11,000 in Sabah, making it an endangered species.

Turtle Islands Marine Park

All year round, green and hawksbill turtles gather to lay their eggs on the island beaches north of Sandakan Bay. The park is 40km (25 miles) from Sandakan and comprises three islands – **Pulau Selingaan**, **Pulau Bakkungan** and **Pulau Gulisaan** – covering 1,740 hectares (4,295 acres). At Pulau Selingaan there are several furnished chalets where up to 20 visitors can stay overnight and maintain their night-long vigil.

West of Lahad Datu

Another access point to the wilds of Sabah is through the **Danum Valley Conservation Area**. The valley is 80km (50 miles) inland from Lahad Datu on Sabah's east coast. Here are a range of walking trails through the protected forests, home to the western tarsier, orang-utan, leopard cat, deer, Malayan sun bear, the very rare Sumatran rhinoceros, smooth otter and 275 species of birdlife. Resort accommodation is available but to visit the wilderness area of the **Maliau Basin Conservation Area**, west of Danum, expect only camping facilities. Nicknamed 'Sabah's Lost World', Maliau Basin was accidentally discovered in 1947 by a British pilot, then promptly forgotten until the first expedition in 1988. Less than half of the basin remains unexplored, but what has been discovered so far is an exciting diversity of flora and fauna, some of which are endemic to this basin. **Imbak Canyon Conservation Area ⓲** is located northeast of Maliau and is unique for its diversity of flora. It serves as the state's botanical gene bank and a water catchment area. A valley 10km (6 miles) long, it is drained by the Imbak River and features beautiful waterfalls, hemmed in from three sides by sandstone ridges. Apply to the Yayasan Sabah (Sabah Foundation) in KK or Sandakan for the visitor's permit, but it is best to go with a reliable tour operator.

Southeast islands of Sabah
Semporna, an hour's drive from Tawau airport, is the gateway to the famous island of **Pulau Sipadan ⓳** – Malaysia's only oceanic island and one of the world's five best dive sites. A pinnacle of limestone and coral rising up 600m (2,000ft) from the floor of the Celebes Sea, it spreads out like a mushroom cap to form a 12-hectare (30-acre) island. To safeguard the underwater reefs, no accommodation is allowed on the island. Instead, visitors stay at nearby Pulau Mabul and Pulau Kapalai, both well known for their underwater macro life.

Orang-utans

In Malay, orang-utan means 'forest person' – an appropriate mark of respect for the mammal biologically closest to man. These intelligent, russet-coloured apes live in the forests of Sabah and Sarawak. They are very individualistic nomads, meeting occasionally to share a fruit supper before going their own way. Some visitors to Sepilok confuse them with the similarly coloured red-leaf monkeys – but unlike monkeys, orang-utans have no tails.

WHAT TO DO

Sightseeing is, of course, only a part of your visit to Malaysia. You will probably want to take time to shop for traditional arts and crafts in Kuching, check out the night markets of Kuala Lumpur, or drop by a few Chinese antiques shops in Penang. Those who wish to can have quite an active holiday simply sampling the local shopping scene. Malaysia offers a showcase of festivals and events throughout the year, as well.

SHOPPING

An excellent variety of goods is available throughout Malaysia. Large department stores and malls are found in most major cities, with night markets offering fresh food and clothing that is very competitively priced. Antique shops brim with traditional handicrafts and Chinese antiques, while batik fabric designs, silver- and pewter-ware and silk brocaded *songket* cloth are popular items.

Away from the major department stores bargaining is expected; but make sure on more expensive items that you have a good idea of retail prices before you begin.

Malaysia's tax havens are the islands of Langkawi, Tioman and Labuan. Duty-free areas are also found at Rantau Panjang and Pengkalan Kubur, both in Kelantan; Padang Besar and Bukit Kayu Hitam in Kedah; and Johor Bahru in Johor. Duty-free shops can also be found at all international airports.

What to buy

Most major towns have **handicraft stores**, like KL's Craft Complex on Jalan Conlay, which act as a showcase for products

Traditional kite flying in Selangor

Batik masks for sale in Melaka's Jonkers Street

from all over the peninsula and East Malaysia. KL's Central Market gives you a wider selection. As far as quality is concerned, some of the best traditional products are found in the **museum shops** in Kuala Lumpur, Melaka, Kuching and Kota Kinabalu. The selection is more comprehensive in the markets and shops of Kelantan, Terengganu, Sarawak and Sabah. In Kota Bharu or Kuala Terengganu, take a guided *kampung* tour to see the artisans at work – you'll often find you can get their products at a better price than in town.

Batik. Bright and enticing, these colourfully patterned fabrics are today both hand- and factory-made in Kelantan and Terengganu, but had their origins in the Malay kingdoms of Java more than 1,000 years ago. The technique remains the same, although it was adopted on the peninsula only in the 20th century. A design of melted wax is applied to cotton or silk, using a *canting*, a traditional hand tool. The fabric is then dipped in cool vegetable or synthetic dye, which colours the cloth around the wax pattern. The piece is then dipped in hot water to remove the wax, leaving a lighter design behind. The process may be repeated for multiple colouring. You can either purchase the cloth and have it tailored back home or buy a sarong – useful at the beach over a bikini. Other items include hats, scarves, ties, purses, shirts and wall-hangings. Do note that the quality of batik can vary greatly.

Kain Songket. *Kain Songket* (silk brocade) is a speciality of Terengganu and Kuching. On a hardwood frame, silver and gold threads are woven into fine silk, usually of emerald green, dark red, purple or royal blue in geometric and floral patterns. *Songket* was originally reserved for royalty, but is today also used for bridal dresses, ceremonial robes, cushion covers and handbags.

Nyonya kebaya and beaded shoes. The traditional attire of the Peranakan (Malay for 'locally born') community in Penang and Melaka is the *sarong kebaya* – a sarong matched with a Malay-like blouse. But the female Chinese Peranakan or Nyonya preferred wearing a figure-hugging blouse intricately embroidered with beautiful designs. The finer the embroidery work, the more costly it is. In Penang's Gurney Plaza, Madam Lim is the doyen of *nyonya kebaya*-making (tel: 04-226 6110). *Kasut Manek*, or beaded shoes, are handmade slippers decorated with colourful motifs, comprising hundreds of tiny glass beads. Match them with either a *nyonya kebaya* or an evening dress. In Melaka, 63 Jalan Tokong has a wide collection of beaded slippers.

A painter at work in KL's Central Market

Weaving by hand

Silverwork and pewter. The silversmith's centuries-old skills, originally developed at the court of Perak, are continued today in rural Kelantan. Besides earrings, brooches, necklaces and bracelets, you will find plaques and filigree jewellery, snuff boxes (originally designed for betel nuts), belt buckles, lacquered trays and magnificent bowls.

Pewter-work, in the form of goblets, tankards, wine carafes, trays and salt- and pepper-shakers, is a luxury side-product of the tin industry. It is actually 95 percent tin, hardened with a 5 percent alloy of antimony and copper. The major names to look out for are Royal Selangor and Tumasek Pewter, both available throughout the country at major department stores. At Royal Selangor's visitor centres in KL (Jalan Usahawan 6), Straits Quay in Penang and Clarke Quay in Singapore you can hammer out your own pewter masterpiece as a keepsake (www.visitorcentre.royalselangor.com). The Tumasek Pewter factory is on Jalan Kuang Bulan in Taman Kepong, KL.

Other craftwork. One of the most attractive products of the traditional arts is the highly decorative **puppet** used in the *wayang kulit* shadow theatre (see page 140). The demons, warriors and kings that you can watch being made in a Kelantan rural workshop can make splendid ornaments.

More practical but quite decorative are bamboo and rattan **baskets** and **mats** woven from nipa palm leaves.

In **Kuching** look for Iban *pua kumbu* (handwoven **blankets**), wooden hornbill carvings used in rituals, and silver

Point of etiquette

Avoid pointing with your fingers, which in Malay culture is considered rude. It is better to extend the flat of your hand in the direction you wish to indicate.

jewellery, woven Bidayuh baskets, Orang Ulu beadwork and woodcarving, and Penan blowpipes and mats. Most antique and curio shops are along Jalan Main Bazaar just beside the waterfront, with a few in the Padungan area.

An authentic **blowpipe** is one of the most accomplished pieces of indigenous craftwork in all of Malaysia. Really good ones are now increasingly rare and quite expensive, and their length, 2m (over 6ft), makes them difficult to carry around. If you cannot stretch to a real hardwood blowpipe, you can buy the handsome quiver of stout, rattan-bound bamboo with the poison darts (minus the poison), both authentic, and a shorter pipe of bamboo that does a perfectly serviceable job of blowing darts into your cork dartboard at home.

Sarawak **pottery** is ochre-coloured with bold geometric designs. Sayong pottery, from Perak, has a glossy black colour. There is even pottery from Johor, decorated with batik and gold thread, giving it a distinctive look.

Antiques. Melaka's Baba Nyonya Chinese quarter (see page 94) is a great place to hunt and bargain for old porcelain imported from southern China and antique silver or jade bracelets. Penang is also popular for antiques-lovers – head for Jalan Pintal Tali (Rope Walk), which offers porcelain-ware, coins, old glass and antique clocks. Occasionally treasures can be unearthed – notably old Chinese theatrical costumes and fake jewellery – as you rummage among the piles of junk in George Town's famous flea market at Lorong Kulit.

Discount and duty-free goods. You can get good deals on **watches**, **jewellery**, major-brand **sports clothes** and **jeans** in the **street markets** of Kuala Lumpur – especially around Chinatown's Jalan Petaling – and of George Town along Jalan Penang, Lebuh Campbell and Lebuh Chulia. Bargaining here is almost compulsory. The fakes are best distinguished from the genuine articles by how low a price the vendor will accept.

The **Little Penang Street Market**, held every last Sunday of the month in Jalan Penang near the Eastern and Oriental Hotel, showcases Penang's culture and creativity with craft and food stalls, performances and visual arts.

There are many excellent and **modern shopping centres** in KL on and around Jalan Bukit Bintang, near the bigger

Straight and narrow blowpipes

Kayan, Kenyah and nomadic Penan hunters make the best *sumpitan* (blowpipes) from coveted Sarawak straight-grained hardwood. From the felled tree, they cut a piece about 2.5m (8ft) long and shave it with an adze to a cylindrical form about 10cm (4in) in diameter. This straight but rough pole is lashed firmly to a series of supports so as to stand perfectly upright. Its upper end projects above a platform where an artisan – with a chisel-pointed iron rod for a drill – slowly and meticulously bores a dead-straight hole down through the pole. The weapon's bore must be as clean and polished as that of a rifle barrel for the dart to pass through unimpeded. Its shaft is shaved, rounded and smoothed to produce a finished blowpipe of about 2.51cm (1in) in diameter.

The pipe often comes with a sharp spear point at its non-blowing end to finish off larger prey that would only have been stunned by the poison in the dart, such as deer, wild pig or, perhaps, in the old days, humans. The poison is made from the sap of the Ipoh tree.

Wayang Kulit shadow theatre

international hotels. These include Lot 10, the Pavilion, KLCC, Starhill Gallery and Low Yat Plaza (electronics). On weekends, Mid Valley Megamall near Bangsar Baru, and Queensbay Mall and Gurney Plaza in Penang are usually very crowded.

ENTERTAINMENT

Nightlife

To cater to Western tastes, the major cities – KL, George Town, Melaka, Johor Bahru, Kuantan, Kuching and Kota Kinabalu – and the beach resorts have nightclubs and cocktail lounges with live music. The jazz and popular music scene is mostly dominated by Filipino performers of very high calibre. The singers deliver stunning carbon-copy renditions of current and past hits, while the musicians are quite brilliant in their set pieces or improvisations.

Traditional dance and theatre

Malaysia's traditional entertainment is more often than not a daytime affair. Tourist information offices in Kota Bharu and Kuala Terengganu can inform you about times and reservations. This information can also be found at the Malaysia Tourism Office in KL.

Mak Yong dance drama. This elegant art form evolved over 400 years ago in the Malay state of Pattani, now part of southern Thailand, and today is performed across the border in Kelantan. It consists of a play on one of a dozen set romantic themes, accompanied by dance, operatic singing and knockabout comic routines. The orchestra of *rebab* (bowed fiddle), *tawak-tawk* (gongs) and *gendang* (double-headed drums) plays music with a distinctly Middle Eastern flavour.

Wayang Kulit shadow theatre. The most popular form of shadow theatre is known as *Wayang Siam*. It is of Malay rather than Siamese origin, drawing on themes from the Hindu epic *Ramayana*. It dates back more than 1,000 years to when Indian merchants first brought their Hindu culture to the peninsula. The stories surrounding Prince Rama and his wife Sita involve ogres, demon-kings and monkey warriors, all represented on stage by puppets. With its customary cheerfulness, Malay culture has added a comic element absent from the high drama of the original.

The small timber and bamboo theatre is mounted on stilts, and the puppets are seen as sharply etched

Festival fun

Malaysians love celebrating, and with so many different religions – Islam, Hinduism, Buddhism, Christianity and aboriginal animism – they give themselves plenty of opportunities. They often join in each other's festivities, Muslims inviting Chinese friends to their Hari Raya feasts to end the fast of Ramadan, and members of all the communities turning up for Melaka's Christian processions at Easter.

Paragliding on Langakawi's Canang Beach

shadows cast on a white cotton screen by a lamp hanging from the roof of the theatre. One *dalang* (puppeteer), accompanied by a band of musicians playing oboes, drums, gongs and cymbals, acts out all the parts and produces all the different voices. He peeps from behind the screen to assess the age and sophistication of his audience and varies the play accordingly. Originally, all the brightly coloured puppets were made from cow, buffalo, or goat hides, but today the minor characters are turned out in plastic and celluloid. The bright colours are said to vary the intensity of the shadows and help differentiate the characters.

SPORTS

Water sports

Most large hotels and resorts have their own **swimming pools**, which are a necessity in the hot climate. The coolest and most exhilarating swim is to be had in the natural pools of the water-falls of Taman Negara and Mount Kinabalu national parks. But if you prefer good sandy **beaches**, head for the east coast. The beaches of Kelantan and Terengganu, especially the near-deserted Rantau Abang, and further south at Johor's Desaru, haven't yet suffered as much from industrialisation as those on the west coast. But Tioman Island has some of the east coast's best beaches, particularly if you like secluded coves. On the west coast, your best bets are the resorts on Penang, Pangkor or Langkawi islands. In Sarawak, the best beaches are northwest of Kuching, at Damai, Santubong or Bako National Park; in Sabah, either at Kota Kinabalu's offshore islands of the Tunku Abdul Rahman Park or up at Kudat on Borneo's northernmost tip; over on Sabah's east coast try the islands off Sandakan Bay.

The resorts offer excellent amenities for all types of water sports: **snorkelling**, **scuba diving**, **windsurfing**, **sailing** and **water-skiing**. Scuba divers should remember that the coral and other marine life are protected species and are not to be touched or damaged.

Other sports

The British have left their mark: the country has more than 250 golf courses, with a choice of 9, 18, 27 and 54 holes. When the local course is private, as at The Royal Selangor Golf Club in KL, your hotel can book on your behalf (weekdays except public holidays, 8.30am–10.30pm). Bring your golf handicap card. The most refreshing courses are in the cooler hill sta-tions, notably Cameron Highlands and Fraser's Hill. The best course is at Saujana Golf and Country Club near KL, but there are pleasant 18-hole courses on Langkawi Island as well (the Datai Bay Golf Club re-opens mid-2013). Golfers say that the best resort course is the Bukit Jambul Golf Club in Penang.

The national sport, **badminton**, is played wherever a net, real or makeshift, can be set up for players to thwack the shuttlecock across to each other. Many resort hotels provide proper courts.

Tennis facilities are also widely available, but the climate makes it a sport best reserved for early morning, or evenings, when the courts are floodlit.

Freshwater **fishing** is a delight in the mountain streams of Taman Negara and Kinabalu parks or on Lakes Bera and Kenyir. Off the east coast, you could try **deep-sea fishing** for barracuda or trevally. In all cases, enquire first at tourist information offices about the necessary fishing permits. **Hunting** licences are so restricted that it is scarcely worth the trouble for ordinary tourists.

Lata Iskandar waterfall in the Cameron Highlands

Traditional Malay sports

Like the arts and crafts, ancient Malay sports and pastimes are practised almost exclusively on the east coast, though you may also see demonstrations elsewhere at cultural centres in KL, Kota Bharu or Sarawak. The best time to see them is in the weeks following the rice harvest and during the special festivals that stage state-wide contests (see page 145).

Kelantan and Terengganu preserve a centuries-old tradition of **flying ornamental kites** measuring 2m (6ft 6ins) across and the same from head to tail. In *kampung* workshops you can watch fantastic birds and butterflies being made of paper (and increasingly of plastic, too) drawn over strong, flexible bamboo frames. Village contests judge competitors on their most spectacular flying skills – height, dexterity and the humming sound produced by the wind through the kite-head.

Like kite flying, **top-spinning** is no mere child's game. Adults can keep a top in motion for over 50 minutes. The top looks somewhat like a discus, made of hardwood with a steel knob or spike in the centre and a lead rim. The standard size is about 23cm (9in) in diameter. It takes some six weeks to complete the construction of what is considered to be a precision instrument. Villages stage team games with the objective of keeping a top spinning for the longest time. Another derivative of the game, using a different kind of top, has for its objective knocking the opponent's top out of the spinning area.

Sepak Takraw is a kind of volleyball played with a ball made of rattan, which the players can hit with every part of their body except hands and forearms. One team has to get over the net to the other team, without being in contact with the ball more than three times on their side of the court. A three-man team scores points each time the ball hits the ground on the opponent's court or if the ball is hit out of the court.

Playing Sepak Takraw

The Malay martial art silat came from Sumatra some 400 years ago. It is performed with elegant stylised gestures, either as a form of wrestling, or as fencing with a sword or a traditional *kris*, known as *pencak silat*.

Calendar of Events

Check precise dates before you leave, as the timing of Malaysia's many festivals tends to vary each year.

January/February. New Year's Day is a national public holiday.
Chinese New Year is a 15-day celebration accompanied by red banners and lion dances in Chinatown. KL, Penang, Kuching and KK are the best places for watching.
Thaipusam is the Hindu festival celebrated with a procession of penitents seeking absolution at his shrine. The biggest is from KL to the Batu Caves (see page 45).

March/April. Easter: Eurasians and indigenous Christian converts celebrate with Good Friday processions, most famously the Portuguese community of Melaka at St Peter's Church.
Petronas F1 Malaysia Grand Prix: catch the second race of the season in Sepang.

May. Kadazans celebrate Tadau Kaamatan (Sabah Rice Harvest Festival).
Borneo Jazz in Miri is an international festival for jazz lovers.
Sabah Fest is a cultural extravaganza in KK featuring food, handicraft and dance performances.
Colours of 1Malaysia, a national celebration of cultural diversity.

June. Dayaks in Sarawak mark Hari Gawai Dayak (Rice Harvest Festival).
Festa de San Pedro (29 June): Christian tribute to Peter, patron saint of fishermen, in Melaka.

July/August. Rainforest World Music Festival in Sarawak.
Hari Raya Aidil-Fitri celebrations mark the end of Ramadan.
Hari Merdeka (Independence Day; 31 August) is a national public holiday.
September. Hari Malaysia (Malaysia Day; 16 September) is a national public holiday.

October/November. Deepavali (Festival of Lights): Major Indian celebration, with candles lit, family feasts and prayers in the temple.
Kota Belud Market Festival, with spectacular movements by Bajau cowboys.

December. Street Food and Restaurant Festival throughout December.
Monsoon Cup attracts sailing competitors to Pulau Duyong.

EATING OUT

A meal in Malaysia can be as varied as the ethnic mix that makes up the country. Chinese, Indian, Indonesian and Thai recipes and ingredients all make their contribution. Malay cuisine itself is often a combination of all these and other ingredients as well.

In addition to hotel restaurants, major cities including Kuala Lumpur, Melaka, Ipoh and Penang's George Town all have high-quality independent Chinese and Indian restaurants and a few Malay ones. Smart-casual dress is all that is required in most. Meal times are also less rigid, especially as the popular hawkers' centres often serve meals all day long. Vegetarians need not worry: many Chinese and Indian shops offer various vegetarian dishes. Many independent restaurants close for one day of the week, usually Monday.

Food Stalls. The arena for a gastronomic adventure is the open-air food court. The stalls line both sides of a street or surround a court filled with tables, each offering different dishes of seafood, meat, chicken, vegetables, barbecue, soup, noodles or rice. Every town has its popular venues: in KL, there are Jalan Alor and Chinatown's Jalan Petaling; in Melaka, Melaka Raya; in Penang, Gurney Drive; in Ipoh, Jalan Yau Tet Shin; in Kota Bharu, Jalan Padang Garong; in Kuching, Lintang Batu.

The right hand

The left hand – and left-hand side – is considered to be impolite, and for Muslims and Indians eating with the left hand is viewed as unclean. Use the right hand for eating, greeting or handing anything to someone.

Find yourself a free table, note its number and begin your round of the hawkers, placing your orders then simply waiting for the

Grilling satay at a Kuala Lumpur hawker stall

various dishes to be brought over to you. Pay in cash when your meal arrives.

In coffee shops without table numbers, hawkers easily recall where you are sitting. If there are no empty tables, most people are willing to share their table with you. Just enquire if the seat is already taken.

WHAT TO EAT

Malay cuisine

Like Indonesian cuisine with which it shares a common tradition, Malay cooking is rice-based, but the southern Chinese influence has also made noodles very popular.

The most common Malay dish is *satay* – pieces of chicken, beef or mutton, sometimes venison (pork being forbidden, of course) skewered and cooked over charcoal. It is served in a spicy sauce of ground peanuts, peanut oil, chillis, garlic, onion,

Tucking into breakfast on Jalan Petaling in Kuala Lumpur

sugar and tamarind water, with slices of cucumber and *ketupat*, glutinous rice wrapped in palm leaves.

Mee rebus is a combination of noodles with beef, chicken or prawns and cubes of bean curd in a piquant brown gravy.

To say that *prawn sambal* is spicy would be an understatement. It is served with *nasi lemak* (rice steamed in coconut milk), chillis and condiments. Malays often eat with their fingers (see page 146), but you will be offered a fork and spoon if you wish.

Tauhu bakar, a soybean cake in a sweet, spicy peanut sauce with cucumber slices, is served on a nest of bean sprouts. Rice seasoned with lemon grass, chillis, ginger and soy accompanies beef *rendang*, pieces of beef marinated in coconut milk.

Otak-otak is a grilled banana-leaf 'packet' of fish paste with coconut. Try *gula melaka sago* (pudding with coconut milk and a syrup of palm sugar), or *cendol* (coconut milk with green jelly and syrup of palm sugar).

Chinese cuisine

With the Chinese community so dominant in many of the towns, you will often find more Chinese than Malay restaurants and food stalls. Along with the staples of Chinese cooking, you will find a wide range of regional dishes in Malaysia.

Hokkien cooking specialises in noodles. Try *Hokkien-fried mee*, moist noodles with prawn, squid, pork and vegetables. Or *chien* is a seasoned omelette with tiny oysters and spring onions. In Klang and KL, Hokkien chefs make excellent *bah kut teh*, a soup of pork ribs, garlic and herbs. *Eight-jewel chicken* or *duck*, which is stewed and boned, is stuffed with diced pork,

Tropical fruit

Malaysia may not be able to match France's 400 cheeses, but it does have 40 different kinds of bananas. The tiny ones are the sweetest, while the big green ones are used for cooking. Connoisseurs sing the praises of the three-panelled rather than the commoner four-panelled banana.

Besides the deliciously sweet watermelon and pineapple, there are some real exotica to be discovered. The largest of all is the huge pear-shaped jackfruit, hanging directly from the tree's trunk and main branches. Nicely tart in taste, the yellow flesh has a chewy consistency.

Without its hairy red skin, the white-fleshed rambutan is almost indistinguishable in taste from the lychee – delicious. The waxy yellow-skinned *carambola* (starfruit) does not look like a star until you cut it in slices. It is refreshingly tangy.

Once you get past the foul smell of durian, it really is very tasty. Addicts say 'Smell? What smell?' Spiky and big as a football, its flesh is rich and creamy, best of all in its wild state in the forest.

If you are a health fanatic, go for the vitamin-packed guava, green-skinned with white flesh, or papaya, green-skinned with orange pulp, or the sensual mango, growing, it seems, in a dozen different varieties in almost every Malaysian's back garden.

Banana leaf curry

mushrooms, dried prawns, carrots and glutinous rice. *Carrot cake* is, in fact, more of an omelette made with a grated radish that the Chinese call 'white carrot'. Also popular is the *popiah*, a rice-flour spring roll of shredded meat, turnip, bean sprouts, bean curd, prawn and garlic.

Teochew cooking is famous for its *steamboat*, a southern Chinese version of fondue – very big on KL's Jalan Petaling. Pieces of fish and seafood, meat, chicken and vegetables are dipped by each diner into hot stock in the bubbling 'steamboat' set in the centre of the table. At the end, the stock makes an excellent soup with which to finish the meal. Teochew cuisine is light and non-greasy, based principally on seafood. The fresh fish is sweet because it is first mixed with a very light concoction of sweet berry sauce, peanuts and sesame oil.

A favourite hawker-stall noodle dish is *char kway teow*, with prawns, cockles, bean sprouts and eggs fried in chilli and dark soy sauce. In Penang, Chinese hawkers sell pork satay.

Hainan Island has contributed the great dish *Hainanese chicken rice*. The steamed chicken is served in pieces with onion-flavoured rice and a special sauce of pounded chillis, lime juice and garlic. You can also try the masterful mutton soup simmered with Chinese herbs, ginger and young bamboo shoots.

Nyonya cuisine

This aromatic and spicy cuisine is a blend of Chinese and Malay traditions developed by descendants of the Chinese who intermarried in the Straits Settlements of Melaka, Penang and Singapore. The result is a much spicier version of the many southern Chinese dishes mentioned above. Most famous in Penang is *Assam laksa*, a hot and sour fish-based noodle soup flavoured with tamarind, lemon grass and curry spices.

Bubur cha cha is a coconut milk creation with pieces of yam, sweet potato, sago and coloured gelatin. The Nyonya version of *otak-otak* is a fish cake with coconut milk, lemon grass and shallots, wrapped in a palm leaf and grilled.

Indian cuisine

The best Indian food stalls serve their curries, rice, fish, meat and vegetables piled high on a broad expanse of banana leaf. Indians also may eat with their fingers (see page 146) but cutlery is available.

Most of Malaysia's Indian community comes from the south of the subcontinent, where the searingly hot curries are sweetened by coconut milk. Chefs in North Indian restaurants tend to use a lot of yoghurt

Local speciality

Walk through any Malaysian town mid-morning and the most crowded eateries will usually be those serving *roti canai*, a deliciously light, flaky pancake served with dhal.

A fish stall at Kota Kinabalu's
waterfront food market

and a more subtle variety of spices. Since World War II, their numbers have been increased by Muslim immigrants from Pakistan and Bangladesh, who have added beef to the traditional mutton and chicken dishes. Many Hindu restaurants, particularly around the temples, are purely vegetarian, offering delicious variations on curried aubergine, tomatoes, potatoes, lentils and okra (lady's fingers), accompanied by traditional breads – *thosai*, *chapati*, *naan*, *roti canai* and, of course, *papadam* (poppodom).

As universal now as Chinese food, the Indian and Indian-Muslim dishes you will come across in Malaysia include *biryani* (rice and meat, fish or vegetables cooked together, with nuts, dried fruit and spices); *tandoori* (marinated pieces of chicken or fish baked in a clay oven); and *murtabak* (rice-dough pancakes, which are folded over chicken, beef or mutton, onion, eggs and vegetables). The latter can be a handy take-away snack but is better eaten at the table dipped in curry gravy.

Drinks

With all those exotic tropical fruits just dropping off the trees, the best drink here is a simple, fresh fruit juice – mango, lime, *carambola* (starfruit), watermelon, guava and pineapple being the most common. Malaysians like soy milk, often sold at markets in a bowl. The same stall would also sell *tau fu fah*, a soy custard sweetened with syrup. One of the cheapest local drinks is coconut water, from green king coconuts.

If you want a local brew, try the potent rice wine in Sarawak and Sabah. *Tuak* is the fermentation, *lankau* the processing with yeast. Imported beers like Heineken and Carlsberg are also available.

TO HELP YOU ORDER...

Could we have a table?	**Boleh dapatkan kami sebuah meja?**
I'd like a/an/some...	**Saya hendak...**
bread	**roti**
butter	**mentega**
cheese	**keju**
coffee	**kopi**
eggs	**telur**
fish	**ikan**
fruit	**buah**
ice	**ais**
ice cream	**ais krim**

meat	**daging**
menu	**menu**
milk	**susu**
mineral water	**air mineral**
potatoes	**ubi kentang**
rice	**nasi**
sugar	**gula**
tea	**teh**
vegetables	**sayur**

...AND READ THE MENU

ais krim	ice cream
anggur	grapes
ayam	chicken
babi	pork
bawang putih	garlic
bola daging	meatballs
cili hijau	green chilli
hati	liver
ikan	fish
kacang	beans
kambing	goat

kastad karamel	caramel custard
limau	lemon
nanas	pineapple
nasi goreng	fried rice
raspberi	raspberries
sayur-sayuran	vegetables
sosej pedas	spicy sausage
stek daging	beefsteak
udang	prawns

PLACES TO EAT

*The price symbols below are intended as a guide, and are based on a
standard meal for two without drinks.*

$$$$ over US$50   **$$$** US$25–50
$$ US$10–25   **$** less than US$10

KUALA LUMPUR, SELANGOR AND PUTRAJAYA

Antipodean Café $$ *20 Jalan Telawi 2, Bangsar Baru, 59100
Kuala Lumpur; tel: 03-2282 0411.* This café offers a wide selec-
tion of hearty and tasty breakfast choices, including pork bacon,
a rarity in this area. After 11am, the menu changes to a healthy
selection of sandwiches, salads and kebabs. It also roasts its own
direct-trade Indonesian Arabica coffee on the premises. Popular
with the locals, Kiwi and Aussie community, it gets crowded on
weekend mornings. Open daily 8am–10pm.

Chat Masala $ *259-G Jalan Tun Sambanthan, Brickfields, 50470
Kuala Lumpur; tel: 03-2260 3244.* Located along Little India's
main road, beside KFC and a 10-minute walk from KL Sentral,
this Indian restaurant serves tasty vegetarian dishes. It also serves
roti canai all day. Open Thu–Tue 7.30am–11.30pm, Wed 3.30pm–
11.30pm.

Jake's $$$ *Feast Floor, Starhill Gallery, Lower Ground Floor, 181
Jalan Bukit Bintang, 55100 Kuala Lumpur; tel: 03-2148 1398.* Im-
ported steaks cooked to perfection are the speciality at this Wild
West-themed restaurant, but the comprehensive menu runs the
gamut from seafood to vegetarian dishes. Open daily noon–1am.

Penang Village $$ *Lot G89, Ground Floor, Alamanda Shopping
Centre, Jalan Alamanda, Presint 1, 62000 Putrajaya; tel: 03-8888
4268.* The signature dishes here are *char kway teow*, *nasi lemak*
with *beef rendang* and oyster omelette. Finish your meal with the
delightful *cendol* or *sago* pudding. Open daily 11.30am–10.30pm.

Real and Wholesome (R.A.W. Coffee) $$ *Ground Floor, Wisma Equity, 150 Jalan Ampang, 50450 Kuala Lumpur; mobile tel: 019-313 8978.* This shop, north of KLCC, is a vegetarian/vegan café serving coffee by Artisan Roast KL. It has a limited breakfast and lunch selection but that will change when the restaurant opens (due in 2013). For a RM2 coffee discount, bring your own tumbler to take away. Open Mon–Fri 7.30am–7.30pm, Sat 9am–6pm.

River View Seafood $$ *1 Jalan Besar, Pasir Penambang, 45000 Kuala Selangor; tel: 03-3289 2238.* This family-run eatery behind Caltex station in Kuala Selangor town serves quality seafood dishes. It is breezy and offers views of the bridge and Bukit Melawati. Open daily 11am–10pm.

PERAK

Indulgence Restaurant and Living $$$ *14 Jalan Raja Dihilir, 30350 Ipoh, Perak; tel: 05-255 7051.* Chef Julie Song's restaurant is in a colonial bungalow and serves modern European cuisine and specials like Australian *wagyu* and Japanese *Kobe* beef. Open Wed–Sun 9am–11.30pm.

Thean Chun Coffee Shop $ *73 Jalan Market (near the Birch Memorial Clock Tower), 30000 Ipoh, Perak; tel: 05-255 3076.* Enjoy Ipoh favourites like *kai see hor fun* (rice noodles in a chicken-prawn stock), Chinese-style satay (skewers of chicken, pork intestines or liver) and fresh *popiah* (like spring rolls) from Kong Heng coffee shop next door. Open Fri–Wed 8am–4.30pm.

CAMERON HIGHLANDS

Restoran Kumar $ *26 Main Road, Tanah Rata, 39000 Cameron Highlands, Pahang; tel: 05-491 2624.* Located near Starbucks, Restoran Kumar serves Indian food at affordable prices, and also caters for vegetarians. Naan, tandoori and banana leaf rice are recommended dishes. Open daily 7am–10pm.

The Smokehouse Hotel & Restaurant $$$ *By the Golf Course, 39000 Tanah Rata, Cameron Highlands, Pahang; tel: 05-491 1215.*

Have your tea with petite sandwiches and freshly baked scones served with home-made strawberry jam and cream in the garden, with views of the peaceful hills. For dinner, try the beef Wellington or roast beef and Yorkshire pudding. Open daily 7.30am–9.30pm.

Tea'ria $ *Sungai Palas Tea Centre, Jalan Gunung Brinchang, 39100 Brinchang, Cameron Highlands, Pahang; tel: 05-496 2096.* With spectacular panoramic views of the surrounding tea plantation, sip tea and snack on a variety of cakes, tarts and scones. Open Tue–Sun 9am–4.30pm.

PENANG

Amelie Café $$ *6 Lebuh Armenian, 10200 George Town, Penang; mobile tel: 012-496 7838.* Next to Cheah Kongsi is this café with very limited seating, hidden behind a plethora of plants. The freshly made pasta and the real-bacon-and-cream-cheese bagel are delicious. The same couple cooks and serves the food, so expect slower service at peak times. Open Tue–Sun 10am–7pm.

Kafe Kheng Pin $ *80 Penang Road/Jalan Sri Bahari, 10200 Penang (near St Francis Xavier Church).* Penang's hawker food is among the best in the country. Various stalls allow you to make a meal of your visit. Dishes like *lobak*, which look like spring rolls and are made from soya skin, are superb. Open Tue–Sun 7am–3pm.

Perut Rumah $$ *17 Jalan Kelawei, 10250 George Town, Penang; tel: 04-227 9917.* Southeast of Wat Chayamangkalaram monastery, this café is in a charming century-old mansion decorated with antique furniture and old photographs. It has a wide selection of *nyonya* dishes, eaten with *nasi ulam*, the aromatic and crunchy herb rice with ground dried shrimp. Open daily 11am–3pm, 6pm–10pm.

Sri Ananda Bahwan $ *66 Jalan Penang, Little India, 10200 George Town, Penang; tel: 04-263 3841.* Near the Chowrasta Market, serving delicious Indian vegetarian food. It also has a non-vegetarian outlet at No. 55, which specialises in banana leaf rice – a set meal that comes with a variety of vegetables, pickles, *papadams* and your choice of curried meat or fish. Open daily 7am–11pm.

Suffolk House Restaurant $$–$$$$ *250 Jalan Air Itam, 10460 Penang; tel: 04-228 3930.* It is an experience to dine in this early-19th-century historical building, Penang's first 'Great House', with its well-manicured lawns. There's a choice of western set meals for lunch, tea or dinner, with the option of à la carte for dinner. It is tucked behind the Methodist Boys School and next door to the Malaysian-German Society (watch out for the small green signpost on the main road). Open daily noon–2.30pm, 2.30pm–5.30pm, 7pm–10.30pm.

LANGKAWI

L'Osteria $$$ *Lot 2863 Jalan Pantai Tengah, 07000 Langkawi, Kedah; tel: 04-955 2133.* For those pining for pizza, pasta and Prosecco, this Italian restaurant dishes up all the popular favourites in comfortable, casual surroundings. While pizzas are popular, other dishes such as *osso bucco* and *tiramisu* are a few of Chef Lorenzo's specialities. Open Tue–Sun 4pm–11pm.

Unkaizan $$$ *Lot 395, Jalan Telok Baru, Pantai Tengah, 07000 Langkawi, Kedah; tel: 04-955 4118.* Enjoy excellent Japanese cuisine in a remote part of the island near the Star Cruise Terminal. Expect the freshest seafood taken live from an in-restaurant tank. Open daily 6pm–11pm, closed on the second Wednesday of each month.

Wonderland Food Store $$ *Lot 179-181, Pusat Perniagaan Kelana Mas, Persiaran Mutiara 2, Kuah, 07000 Langkawi, Kedah; mobile tel: 012-494 6555.* This riverside eatery behind the Bella Vista Hotel is very popular for its good-value Cantonese seafood. Try the stir-fried fresh greens with garlic, oyster egg omelette, squid stir-fried with dried chilli, and shrimp in batter cooked in a spicy tamarind sauce. Pork-free. Open daily 6pm–11.30pm.

PERLIS

Warung Pokok Sawa $ *Kampung Kersik, Mata Ayer, 02500 Kangar, Perlis; mobile tel: 017-393 2006.* This place serves authentic Malay cuisine, but the regulars come for the *ikan bakar* (barbecued fish). Try the signature deep-fried catfish. From Kangar town, follow Persiaran Jubli Emas east towards Arau town. Before the Kubang Gajah primary school turn left onto Route 9. From this junction, head north for 3.5km (2 miles). The stall is on the left after Kampung Mata Ayer. Open Sat–Thu 11.30am–4pm.

KELANTAN, TERENGGANU AND PAHANG

Madam Bee's Kitchen $ *177 Jalan Kampung Cina, 21100 Kuala Terengganu, Terengganu; mobile tel: 012-988 7495.* Located in Chinatown, the Terengganu Peranakan cuisine here is blended with Kelantanese *budu* sauce with an emphasis on spice and seafood. Try the *laksa Terengganu* (noodles in a creamy coconut gravy) and its signature dish – *rojak cerenang* – a fruit salad served with fish crackers in a Chinese gravy. Open Thu–Tue 9.30am–5pm.

Restoran Capital $ *3282 Jalan Post Office Lama (near the Grand Riverview Hotel), 15000 Kota Bharu, Kelantan.* Regular customers queue patiently for the speciality dish – *nasi dagang* (brown rice served on paper with your choice of meat, often a curry). Opens daily from 7am until the food runs out, around 11am. Pork-free.

Terminal Satay Zul $ *A2600 Jalan Alor Akar, 25250 Kuantan Pahang.* Zul started selling satay from the back of his motorcycle in 1974. With his son now at the helm, his succulent chicken, beef, mutton or venison served with piquant sweet peanut sauce and *nasi impit* (compressed rice) – is still doing a roaring trade. Watch out for this corner shop after the river on the left side of Jalan Teluk Sisek as you approach Jalan Alor Akar. Open daily 6pm–12.30am.

NEGERI SEMBILAN

Aunty Aini's Garden Café $$ *Batu 16, Jalan Sepang, Kampung Chelet, 71800 Nilai, Negeri Sembilan; tel: 06-7991276.* Pay a visit here for authentic Minangkabau cuisine (from Sumatra, Indonesia). Try the *sambal belacan & ulam* (herb salad with chilli prawn paste) and the *gulai masak lemak daging salai* (smoked meat cooked in coconut curry). The café is on the right-hand side of the road after Nilai old town, heading towards Sepang. Open Mon–Thu 11.30am–3pm, 5.30pm–11.30pm, Fri–Sat 11.30am–3pm, 5.30pm–12.30am.

MELAKA

Amy Heritage Nyonya Cuisine $$ *75 Jalan Melaka Raya 24, Taman Melaka Raya; tel: 06-286 8819.* While Penang's *nyonya* food is Thai influenced, Melaka's *nyonya* cuisine derives its flavours from the Malay, Chinese and Chitty communities. Try *udang goreng assam* (stir-fried prawns in tamarind paste), *chicken pongteh* (stew) and the *telur dadar cincaluk* (spicy omelette with fermented shrimp paste). Open Tue–Sun 11.30am–2pm, 6pm–9.30pm.

Nasi Ayam Hoe Kee $ *4, 6, 8 Jalan Hang Jebat, 75200 Melaka; tel: 06-283 4751.* Melaka is famous for its Hainan chicken rice ball and the version served here is thought one of the city's best. Dine on steamed chicken, Assam fish curry and lotus root soup. To avoid the long queue, come before noon. Open Mon–Fri 9.30am–5.30pm, Sat and Sun until 7pm. Closed last Wed of the month.

Restaurante San Pedro $$ *4 D'Aranjo Road, Portuguese Settlement, Ujong Pasir, 75050 Melaka; tel: 06-2842170.* This restaurant serves authentic Portuguese cuisine. Try the baked fish (seabass or red snapper), curry *debal* chicken (can be quite spicy), fried *brinjals* and the black pepper crabs. Call ahead to reserve a table (and your fish), because once their stock of fish runs out, they will close for the day. Open Thu–Tue 5.30pm–10pm.

JOHOR BAHRU

Chez Papa French Bistro $$$ *38-40 Jalan Jaya, Taman Maju Jaya, 80400 Johor Bahru, Johor; tel: 07-333 4988.* Excellent food and friendly service make this a favourite. The signature dish is its sirloin steak with pepper cream sauce. It is located southeast of KSL City Shopping Mall, off Tebrau Highway. Open Mon–Sat 6pm–10.30pm and 5.30pm–midnight for drinks and tapas.

KUCHING

Chong Choon Café $ *Lot 121 Jalan Abell, 93100 Kuching, Sarawak.* This simple café near the Tun Jugah Shopping Centre serves the best Sarawak *laksa*. The broth is made from coconut milk and spices and has a sour taste. Noodles, omelette strips and prawns complete the dish. Although open daily from 6.30am to noon, it usually sells out by 11am. Do try the other Sarawakian speciality – *mee kolok*, noodles tossed in a light sauce with shredded chicken or beef. Days off are not fixed.

Steakhouse $$$ *Hilton Kuching, 1 Jalan Tunku Abdul Rahman, 93100 Kuching, Sarawak; tel: 082-223 888.* This smart restaurant has pleasant river views from the window tables and the international menu satisfies the palates of discerning diners. Grilled meat dishes feature but there are also selections of seafood, lamb and prawns. The service is friendly and helpful and there is a good wine list too. Open daily 6pm–10.30pm.

MIRI

Zest $$$$ *Miri Marriott Resort & Spa, Jalan Temenggong Datuk Oyong Lawai, 98000 Miri; Sarawak, tel: 085-421 121.* This open kitchen overlooks the pool. Breakfast and lunch buffets are excellent and buffets are also available in the evening on most weekends. Enjoy Asian and Italian favourites, including freshly made pizza.

KOTA KINABALU

Coast Restaurant and Bar $$$$ *Shangri-la's Rasa Ria Resort, Pantai Dalit, 89208 Tuaran, Sabah; tel: 088-792 888.* With a great location on the beach, the Coast serves contemporary western and vegetarian cuisine flavoured with wild herbs, plants and fruit sourced in Sabah. Indoor dining is available or, if you prefer, sit on the outdoor terrace or in a private thatched gazebo, both with fine views of Borneo's beautiful sunset. Dress code applies. Open daily 6.30pm–10.30pm.

Liew Chai Vegetarian $ *Lot S24 Basement, 1 Jalan Centre Point, 88000 Kota Kinabalu, Sabah; mobile tel: 012-833 7768.* Liew Chai attracts a local crowd to the buffet-style spread of curried or stir-fried vegetables, tofu and mock meat (some dishes may contain eggs). The stall is in the Wan Chai Food Corner of Centre Point Sabah, a shopping mall within walking distance of the waterfront. Open daily 8.15am–6.45pm.

A–Z TRAVEL TIPS

A Summary of Practical Information

A

ACCOMMODATION (see also Budgeting for Your Trip)

Book at least two months in advance during the high season (See Public Holidays) and school holidays (a week in January/February, a week in March, three weeks in June, a week in August and five weeks in November/December). Weekend and holiday surcharges usually apply. The rest of the year is low season and discounts are often available. Island accommodation off the east coast is usually closed during the northeast monsoon months (Nov to Feb/March).

Hotels. International-standard hotels can be found in the state capitals and popular holiday spots. For details, visit the Malaysian Association of Hotels website (www.hotels.org.my).

Budget rooms and chalets. These can be found in resort islands like Langkawi, Pangkor and Tioman, and along East Coast beaches like Cherating, Rantau Abang and Marang.

Guesthouses and apartments. Privately owned, breakfast is usually included and most owners also help with travel arrangements.

Homestays. In villages and longhouses, tourists stay with their host families and participate in daily activities. Check with Homestay Malaysia (www.go2homestay.com).

Resthouses. These are bungalows formerly owned by English planters and civil servants, now turned into hotels with a colonial atmosphere. You will find them in the Cameron Highlands, Taiping, Fraser's Hill and some small towns.

AIRPORTS (see also Getting There)

The major international airports are in Sepang (Kuala Lumpur International Airport or KLIA), Selangor, Subang (the Sultan Abdul Aziz Airport), Bayan Lepas in Penang, Kuching in Sarawak, Labuan Island (an offshore financial centre off Sabah), and Kota Kinabalu in Sabah. You can also fly into Malaysia via Langkawi Island and Tioman Island.

Kuala Lumpur International Airport (KLIA) (KUL; www.klia. com.my; tel: 03-8777 8888) is 70km (43 miles) from KL and connected to KL Sentral rail hub by the high-speed rail link ERL, a 28-minute ride for RM35. From KLIA, the first train is at 5am and last train at 1am (12.30am from KL Sentral); they run every 15–20 minutes. All-day transfers are also available by limousine or taxi. The cost varies depending on where you want to go. To KL City Centre (KLCC), the budget taxi costs RM74, more by limo, luxury car or van. A surcharge of 50 percent applies from midnight to 6am. The Airport Coach from KLIA to KL runs from 12.30am–11pm, departing every 30 minutes for RM18 return. The journey from the city takes up to one hour even with the excellent expressway system and the vehicle travelling at the maximum 110km/h (69mph) speed limit.

Located about 20 km (12 miles) from KLIA is the Low Cost Carrier Terminal (LCCT) (KUL; lcct.klia.com.my; tel: 03-8777 6777) for budget airlines. Feeder buses running at 20-minute intervals link the two terminals. There is also a coach/ERL service to KL Sentral for RM12.50 (7.20am–12.30am; every 30 minutes) or the SkyBus to KL Sentral (3am–10pm; every 30 minutes) for RM9 or to 1-Utama, a shopping centre in Petaling Jaya (5.45am–7.45pm; every 90 minutes) for RM15. Allow 75 minutes' travelling time for these options. You can also purchase a taxi coupon at the arrival hall (generally the same cost as taxis from KLIA to KLCC).

Billed as the world's largest purpose-built terminal for low-cost carriers, KLIA2 (located 2km/1.2 miles from KLIA) is scheduled to take over flights from LCCT from April 2013.

Sultan Abdul Aziz Shah Airport (SAASA) (SZB; www.subang skypark.com/terminal; tel: 03-7845 1717), 26km (16 miles) from KL, is now largely used for private charters, Berjaya Air's flights to various resort islands and Firefly's to domestic and regional airports. Taxis operate 7am to the last arriving flight and, depending on traffic conditions, takes 30–45 minutes to reach KLCC. Costs range from RM40 for a budget taxi to RM70 for a premier taxi and RM80 for a van.

B

BUDGETING FOR YOUR TRIP

Holders of the International Student Identity Card (ISIC), the International Youth Travel Card (IYTC) and Hostelling International receive discounts at selected attractions and hotels.

Flights: A flight from KL to Kuching in Sarawak or Kota Kinabalu in Sabah can cost RM300–600, depending on when you fly and how far in advance you purchase your ticket. From time to time Malaysia Airlines, AirAsia and Firefly have online promotions, offering seat prices under RM50 (before the add-ons) for domestic destinations but for specific dates of travel.

Accommodation. Prices generally start from RM30 a night in budget places (air-conditioning, with a shared bath) to RM130 for a mid-range en-suite double room and RM450 for high-end establishments.

Meals. Food in Malaysia is relatively inexpensive, and, apart from high-end restaurants, you can eat well on a very modest budget. A three-course meal in a mid-range restaurant costs RM30–90.

Museum/attraction entry fees. Nominal admission charges of under RM5 may apply for national and state museums. Private museums charge a higher fee of RM10–20. Entrance to most galleries is free. Zoos and bird parks have higher entry charges, ranging from RM20–45.

C

CAMPING

There is no organised network for campers but camping is a good and cheap option in Malaysia. If you have your own camping gear, campsites with basic facilities such as cooking areas and bathrooms are available within the major nature parks. Charges for park entrance and a hiking permit apply, generally from RM5–30. Some popular camping sites are found at:

Bako National Park, Sarawak: National Parks Booking Office, Visitors Information Centre, Jalan Tun Abang Haji Openg, 93000 Kuching, Sarawak; tel: 082-248 088; www.sarawakforestry.com/htm/snp-np.html.

Endau-Rompin National Park, Johor: Johor National Parks Corporation, Level 1, Bangunan Dato' Mohamad Salleh Perang, Kota Iskandar, 79575 Nusajaya, Johor; tel: 07-266 1301; www.johorparks. johordt.gov.my.

Taman Negara, Pahang: Mutiara Taman Negara, Kuala Tahan, 27000 Jerantut, Pahang; tel: 09-266 3500; www.mutiarahotels.com.

CAR HIRE (see also Driving)

Several car hire companies have counters at most airports, including: KLIA, Penang, Ipoh, Johor Bahru, Kuantan, Kuching, Kota Kinabalu, Bintulu, Miri and Langkawi.

Rates range from RM100–1,000 per day, depending on the make and engine capacity of the car, and whether it is the peak season. Major credit cards are accepted and you are required to leave a refundable deposit. The car will usually be delivered with a full tank of petrol and must be filled up before you hand it back. You need either an international driving licence or a valid licence from your own country (valid for at least one year). In most cases, drivers must be over 21 years of age.

Avis Car Rental: Crowne Plaza Mutiara Kuala Lumpur, Main Lobby, Jalan Sultan Ismail, 50250 Kuala Lumpur; tel: 03-2144 4487; www.avis.com.my.

Extra Rent-A-Car: 2nd Floor, Beverley Hotel, Jalan Kemajuan, 88000 Kota Kinabalu, Sabah; tel: 088-218 160; www.e-erac-online. com.

Kasina Rent-a-Car: 195 Block G, Mukim 12, Jalan Sultan Azlan Shah, Sungai Tiram, Bayan Lepas, 11900 Penang; tel: 04-644 1842; www.kasina.com.my.

Orix Car Rental: Lot 8, Ground Floor, The Federal Hotel Kuala Lumpur, 35 Jalan Bukit Bintang, 55100 Kuala Lumpur; tel: 03-2142 3009, www.orixauto.com.my.

Sime Darby Rent A Car: Lot 2 Ground Floor, Kompleks Antara-

bangsa, Jalan Sultan Ismail, 50250 Kuala Lumpur; tel: 03-2148 6433;
www.simedarbycarrental.com.

CLIMATE

Malaysia is a tropical country, and the heat and humidity can take its
toll on the unsuspecting, especially if you have just departed from
a country in the midst of winter. Daily lowland temperatures range
from 22–35°C (72–95°F). Rainfall averages 250cm (98in) annually.
Nights can be cool.

Monsoon rains bring heavy showers. The northeast monsoon
lasts from November until February; most affected are the east coast
states of Kelantan, Terengganu and Pahang, and parts of Sabah. Some
parts of the country may become isolated during the monsoon, but
this is usually only temporary.

It is not advisable to swim in the sea or travel in small boats off the
east coast during the northeast monsoon. Other than that, the seas in
Malaysia are generally for swimming, sailing and water sports.

CLOTHING (see also Religion)

Since the climate is hot, humid and wet, you should wear thin, light-
coloured, loose clothing, preferably made of cotton. At the hill resorts,
a sweater will suffice to keep you warm but bring warmer clothing
and even gloves if you are visiting Gunung Mulu or Kinabalu.

Malaysians dress in a relaxed manner, even at fancy restaurants. At
a formal occasion, a suit and tie or a long-sleeved batik shirt will do.
However, sandals and slippers are too casual for restaurants and clubs.
At the beach, anything goes except for topless or nude sunbathing.

CRIME AND SAFETY (see also Emergencies and Police)

Malaysia is generally safe, but as in any other country, some basic rules
apply. Petty theft occurs in tourist areas, pickpocketing in crowded
shopping centres and on trains during peak hours and some consular
warnings point to a high rate of credit card fraud and snatch thieves.

If you are a victim of crime, make a report at the nearest Tourist Police (see Emergencies) or police station (tel: 999 from a fixed line) and contact your embassy or consulate if you have lost your passport.

D

DISABLED TRAVELLERS

Basic disabled-friendly facilities, like extra-wide parking bays, wheelchair ramps and toilets, can be found in major hotels, malls, theatres, fast-food chains and some government buildings in the bigger cities like Kuala Lumpur. The Kuala Lumpur International Airport and the Light Rail Transit (LRT) system in Kuala Lumpur are also disabled-friendly. But in general, Malaysia falls short on accommodating people with disabilities. Urban streets are uneven and sometimes potholed and difficult to navigate, while ramps are not that common. Taxis will usually not transport people in wheelchairs or will apply additional charges.

DRIVING (see also Transport)

In Malaysia, driving is on the left – a legacy of British colonialism – and the wearing of seat belts is compulsory. Road signs are in Malay, but in Kuala Lumpur, major tourist destinations are also in English.

The highway code is of the universal type, with distances and speed limits in kilometres. The speed limit varies with the road conditions: it ranges from 90 to 110 km/h (56–68 mph) on highways and from 30 to 80 km/h (18–50 mph) in urban areas and town limits. It is illegal to use mobile phones while driving.

Roads are generally of good quality, and the North–South Expressway, which links Singapore to Thailand, is of international standard, though you have to pay a toll to use it. Rental car companies usually provide you with an emergency contact number should your car break down. Failing that, the Automobile Association of Malaysia (AAM) has a prompt breakdown service for members (tel: 03-2161 0808).

E

ELECTRICITY

The voltage is 220–240 volts throughout Malaysia. Electricity is widely available except in remote areas and some islands, where generators are used.

Note: You will find square three-pin plugs, while some old hotels use two-pin plugs. A universal adapter is handy.

EMBASSIES AND CONSULATES

Unless otherwise noted, all are in Kuala Lumpur.

Australia. 6 Jalan Yap Kwan Seng; tel: 03-2146 5555; www.malaysia. embassy.gov.au.

Canada. 17th Floor, Menara Tan & Tan, 207 Jalan Tun Razak; tel: 03-2718 3333; www.canadainternational.gc.ca.

Ireland. Ireland House, The Amp Walk, 218 Jalan Ampang; tel: 03-2161 2963; www.embassyofireland.my.

New Zealand. 21st Floor, Menara IMC, 8 Jalan Sultan Ismail; tel: 03-2078 2533; www.nzembassy.com.

South Africa. Suite 22.01, Menara HLA, 3 Jalan Kia Peng; tel: 03-2170 2400; www.sahighcomkl.com.my.

UK. 185 Jalan Ampang; tel: 03-2170 2200; www.ukinmalaysia.fco. gov.uk.

US. 376 Jalan Tun Razak; tel: 03-2168 5000; malaysia.usembassy.gov.

EMERGENCIES (see also Crime and Safety)

Dial 999 if you need to contact the police or ambulance services, or 994 for the fire and rescue services.

You'll find Tourist Police in **Kuala Lumpur** (109 Jalan Ampang, 50450 Kuala Lumpur; tel: 03-2163 4422; open 24 hours); **Penang** (Penang Island Contingent Police Headquarters, Jalan Penang, 10500 Penang; tel: 04-222 1728; open Mon–Fri 8am–5pm); **Melaka** (tel: 06-288 3732; Lot 71, Jalan Laksamana, 75000 Melaka; open 24 hours; opposite the Post Office); **Kota Kinabalu** (Sabah Contingent Police Headquarters, Jalan Pahlawan, Kepayan, 88560 Kota Kinabalu; tel: 088-450 222; open Mon–Fri 8am–5pm; opposite the Penang Bazaar) and **Kuching** (Sarawak Contingent Police Headquarters, Jalan Badruddin, 93400 Kuching; tel: 082-250 522; open daily 8am–midnight; a 15-minute walk southwest of Sarawak Museum).

G

GAY AND LESBIAN TRAVELLERS

Homosexuality is illegal under Malaysian law. Nevertheless, gay life is tolerated throughout the country, although discretion is strongly advised, especially in popular meeting places. For further information on this subject, visit www.utopia-asia.com/tipsmala.htm.

GETTING THERE (see also Airports)

Flying is the most common means of getting to Malaysia, with KLIA and LCCT (budget airline terminal) being the major gateways. The national airline, Malaysia Airlines, flies from numerous destinations around the world. Many airlines, like KLM, Singapore Airlines and Cathay Pacific, fly to KLIA. Budget airline AirAsia also connects to the region and internationally to the Middle East, South Asia, Australia and New Zealand. Community airline Firefly also connects to Singapore and selected cities in Thailand and Indonesia. Fares are best booked online. Many people travel to Malaysia quite economically on packages or tours. You can also travel by train or coach from Thailand and Singapore.

GUIDES AND TOURS

Tours or treks into the more remote parts of the country do benefit from the assistance of a guide. Most people make arrangements in advance of their trip but if you have not done so, you can find tour companies in major destinations. Here is a selection:

Borneo Adventure (tel: 082-245 175; www.borneoadventure.com)

provides tours in Sabah and Sarawak.

Dev's Adventure Tours (mobile tel: 019-494 9193; www.langkawi-nature.com) has eco-friendly tours of Langkawi's culture and nature.

Green John Chan (mobile tel: 016-356 9169; www.facebook.com/greenjohnchan) offers trips to destinations steeped in nature, heritage and culture, led by a licensed nature guide.

Hook, Line and Sinker (tel: 03-7725 2551; www.hook-line-sinker.net) has sea fishing and freshwater fishing packages.

NKS Travel (tel: 03-2072 0336; www.taman-negara-nks.com) brings guests from KL to explore Taman Negara.

North Borneo Safari (tel: 089-235 525; www.northborneosafari.com) organises photo safari tours in Borneo.

Ping Anchorage Travel and Tours (tel: 03-4280 8030; www.pinganchorage.com.my) arranges domestic tours.

Riverbug (tel: 088-260 501; www.traversetours.com) has white-water kayaking trips in Sabah's scenic Kiulu and Padas rivers.

TYK Adventure Tours (tel: 088-232 821; www.tykadventuretours.com) offers cycling and World War II tours.

H

HEALTH AND MEDICAL CARE

Every town has a government hospital and major towns and cities have private clinics and hospitals.

If you have a sensitive stomach, do be cautious when ordering food and drink from hawkers' stalls. Though the tap water is chlorinated, drink boiled or bottled water.

Pharmacies, many of which are in department stores, close at 9.30pm. A licensed pharmacist is usually on duty weekdays from 10am–5pm.

Check with your doctor before you travel whether any vaccinations or other health precautions are recommended for your trip. If you have visited a yellow-fever-infected country recently, check the latest regulations about showing an appropriate vaccination certificate.

L

LANGUAGE

Bahasa Malaysia, or Malay, is the national language. But English is widely known and used as well; there shouldn't be any communication problems unless you are in a remote area.

Where is the … consulate?	**Dimanakah konsulat …?**
Do you speak English	**Bolehkah awak bercakap bahasa Inggeris**
I don't understand.	**Saya tidak faham.**
You're welcome.	**Sama-sama.**
Excuse me (I'm sorry).	**Maafkan saya.**
How are you?	**Apa khabar?**
Very well, thank you	**Sangat baik, terima kasih.**
good morning	**selamat pagi**
good evening	**selamat petang**
good night	**selamat malam**
goodbye	**selamat tinggal**
please	**tolong**
thank you	**terima kasih**
yes (correct)	**betul**
no (incorrect)	**salah**
road/street	**jalan/lebuh**
hill	**bukit**
church	**gereja**
temple	**kuil**
mosque	**masjid**
palace	**istana**
park	**taman**

M

MAPS

You can find free maps at hotels, tourist information centres, major airports and train stations. More detailed maps can be purchased at petrol stations and leading bookshops.

MEDIA

Local English-language newspapers are *New Straits Times*, *The Malay Mail*, *The Star* and *The Sun*, available at all newsstands, with *The Sun* being free. In Sabah and Sarawak you will also find local English-language editions of *New Sabah Times*, *New Sarawak Tribune* and *The Borneo Post*. *Juice*, *Vision KL*, and *KLue*, which are some of the popular local lifestyle and entertainment magazines, have news and listings of what is happening in the cities.

MONEY

The official name for the monetary unit is Ringgit Malaysia (RM). One hundred sen make one Ringgit. *Coins:* 5, 10, 20 and 50 sen coins. *Banknotes:* RM1, RM5, RM10, RM20, RM50 and RM100.

Banks and currency exchange. Major credit cards can be used at most hotels, department stores and some shops. Currency can be exchanged at banks or licensed moneychangers (most licensed moneychangers close by 9.30pm if they are in shopping centres). Exchange rates vary, so shop around, but you usually get a better rate at the moneychangers.

O

OPENING TIMES

Malaysia has a dual system regarding the opening hours of government offices. In the states of Kelantan, Terengganu and Kedah, government offices open Sun–Wed 8am–4.15pm, Thu 8am–12.45pm. Banks open Sun–Wed 9.15am–4.30pm, Thu 9.15am–4pm.

For the rest of the country, most banks are open Mon–Thu 9.30am–4.30pm, Fri 9.30am–4pm. Selected banks in shopping centres remain open on weekends or just Saturday 9.15am–12.15pm, while at airports and at KL Sentral, banks are open daily but with different opening hours. Government offices open Mon–Fri 8am–4.15pm, with lunch 12.45pm–2pm except for Friday, when it is prayer time for Muslims 12.30pm–2.45pm.

Shops open daily from 9am until 6 or 7pm, while major department stores open from 10am until 9.30 or 10pm. Most museums close at 5.30pm.

P

POLICE (see also Crime and Safety)

Police stations can be found in almost every city and town in Malaysia. While the policemen and women wear dark-blue uniforms, the Tourist Police wear a chequered hatband with a red-and-blue badge with the letter "I" (for information) on the breast pocket. The federal police headquarters is at Jalan Bukit Aman, Perdana Botanical Gardens, 50480 Kuala Lumpur. Dial 999 for the police.

POST OFFICES

Branches of the General Post Office, or Pos Malaysia, in KL are open Mon–Sat 8am–6pm, Sun 10am–4pm (www.pos.com.my). Those in other towns are open Mon–Sat 8am–5pm, except in Kelantan, Kedah, Perlis and Terengganu, where they are mostly closed on Friday and open on Sunday. Post offices also open on Sundays in Penang (noon–4pm) and Ipoh (9.30am–5pm). Stamps are sold at post offices and hotels, but letters can be dropped into red post boxes found everywhere. Major hotels will post letters for you.

Malaysia has an express mail system (available at major post offices) called Pos Laju, which offers domestic delivery within 24 hours; other express services operate to overseas destinations.

PUBLIC HOLIDAYS

Malaysia has numerous public holidays, which vary from year to year and are as follows:

1 January	New Year's Day
January/February	Chinese New Year (two days)
	Hindu festival of Thaipusam
	Federal Territory Day (in Kuala Lumpur, Putrajaya and Labuan)
March/April	Good Friday (in Sabah and Sarawak)
1 May	Labour Day
May	Wesak Day, a time of prayer for Buddhists
30–31 May	Kaamatan Harvest Festival in Sabah
1–2 June	Gawai Harvest Festival in Sarawak
2 June	King's Birthday
31 August	National Day
16 September	Malaysia Day
November	Hindu festival of Deepavali (except Sabah and Sarawak)
25 December	Christmas Day

There are several public holidays that do not fall on a set date: the Muslim festival of Hari Raya Aidil Fitri (two days), Prophet Mohammed's Birthday, Hari Raya Haji and Awal Muharram.

Malaysians working in urban areas traditionally return to their villages (a practice called *balik kampung*) to celebrate festivals like Chinese New Year, Hari Raya Aidil Fitri and Deepavali. Try not to travel during these *balik kampung* periods as traffic becomes very congested.

R

RELIGION

You should remove your shoes on entering a mosque, or Buddhist or Hindu temple, as shoes are considered to bear the impurities of the outside world. In any case, you should not enter places of worship dressed for the beach. Muslims lend covering robes for women who are bare-shouldered or wearing shorts or skirts above the knees. Food taboos are less strictly imposed, but you should avoid ordering a pork dish when dining with Muslims or beef with Hindus. However, it is acceptable to eat in the presence of Muslims during the fasting month of Ramadan. There is no restriction on photography at places of worship, but discretion is important as some worshippers may not like being photographed.

T

TELEPHONES

Telephone cards are available, and some public phones can be used only with such cards. Coin-operated telephones still exist, but these are for local calls only. International calls can be made at major hotels or by purchasing a prepaid IDD card like iTalk at a 7-11 convenience store.

Calling Malaysia from abroad: To call a fixed-line number in Kuala Lumpur, e.g. 03-xxxx xxxx, dial the international dialling code + country code 60 + area code 3 + number. To call a Malaysian mobile number, say 012-xxx xxxx, dial the international dialling code + country code 60 + 12-xxx xxxx.

Calling locally: If you are calling from within the state, omit the area code; if you are calling another state, dial the area code first. From a Malaysian mobile number, always dial the area code.

Calling internationally: From Malaysia, dial 00 + country code + area code + number. To dial Singapore, dial the access code 02, followed by the number. As prepaid network providers have their own methods to make calls from mobile phones, refer to the booklet that came with your SIM starter pack.

Mobile phone usage: Roaming charges are often very expensive; if you plan to stay in the country longer than a week, and want to make and receive local and international calls, purchase a local or micro SIM card from Maxis, DiGi or Celcom. Starter packs cost up-wards of RM8.50 and come with limited airtime credit.

TIME ZONES

Malaysian time is eight hours ahead of GMT, so when it is 1pm in Kuala Lumpur in July, it is 6am (BST) in London, 1am in New York, 3pm in Sydney, 5pm in Auckland and 7am in Johannesburg.

TIPPING

Tipping is not encouraged, but some tourist drivers and guides may want a reward. At major restaurants and hotels, a 10 percent service charge (plus 6 percent government tax) is added.

TOILETS

Public toilets are not always clean and often do not provide tissue paper; many are also in a state of disrepair. Be prepared to use squat toilets if you are not staying in Western-style establishments. Shopping complexes in KL and major towns normally charge for the use of toilets (20–30 sen; premium toilets RM2); these are much cleaner, and tissue paper is sold at the counter. Toilets at rest areas along the North–South Expressway provide paper, are free and generally clean. Toilets (*bilik air* in Malay) are identified by universal icons and in Malay – *perempuan* (ladies) and *lelaki* (gentlemen).

TOURIST INFORMATION *(Maklumat Pelancong)*

Tourism Malaysia (www.tourism.gov.my) is the main national tourism authority.
Offices of Tourism Malaysia exist in the countries listed below:
Australia. Level 2, 171 Clarence Street, Sydney, NSW 2000; tel: 02-9299 4441; www.tourismmalaysia.com.au
Canada. 1590–1111 West Georgia Street, Vancouver BC V6E 4M3; tel: 604-689 8899; www.tourismmalaysia.ca
Ireland. Embassy of Malaysia: Level 3A Shelbourne House, Shel-

bourne Road, Ballsbridge, Dublin 4; tel: 01-237 6242.

New Zealand. Level 10, DLA Phillips Fox Tower, 205–209, Queen Street, Auckland; tel: 09-309 6290; www.tourismmalaysia.co.nz

South Africa. 1st Floor, Building 5, Commerce Square, 39 Rivonia Road, Sandhurst, Johannesburg 2132; tel: 11-268 0292.

United Kingdom. 57 Trafalgar Square, London WC2N 5DU; tel: 079-307 932; www.facebook.com/pages/Tourism-Malaysia-UK/1018 68413183485.

US. 818 West Seventh Street, Suite 970, Los Angeles, CA 90017; tel: 213-689 9702; www.tourismmalaysiausa.com. 120 East 56th Street, 15th floor, New York, NY 10022; tel: 212-745 1113; www.tourism malaysiany.com

In Malaysia, there are several Tourist Information Offices (www.tourism.gov.my):

Kuala Lumpur. Kuala Lumpur Sentral Station, Lot 21, Level 2, Arrival Hall, Kuala Lumpur City Air Terminal, Stesen KL Sentral; tel: 03-2272 5823; open daily 9am–6pm. Malaysia Tourist Centre (MaTiC), 109 Jalan Ampang; tel: 03-9235 4848/00; open daily 8am–10pm.

Langkawi. Lot SB-2S, Satellite Building, Jetty Point Complex, Kuah; tel: 04-966 7789; open daily 9am–5pm. Langkawi International Airport; Jalan Padang Matsirat; tel: 04-955 7155; open daily 9am until last arriving flight.

Melaka. Jalan Kota, Banda Hilir (opposite the Dutch Square at the roundabout); tel: 06-281 4803; open daily 9am–6pm.

Penang. 11 Lebuh Pantai (next to AmBank), George Town; tel: 04-261 0058; open Mon–Fri 8am–5pm, closed for lunch 1pm–2pm.

Sabah. Terminal 1, Lapangan Tebang Antarabangsa Kota Kinabalu, Jalan Lapangan Terbang (Baru), 88200 Kota Kinabalu; tel: 08-841 3359; open daily 8am–11pm.

Sarawak. Parcel 297-2-1, Level 2, Riverbank Suite, Jalan Tunku Abdul Rahman, 93100 Kuching; tel: 08-224 6575/775; open Mon–Fri 8am–5pm. It also has a counter at the Kuching International Airport, Level 1; open daily 9am–10pm.

TRANSPORT (see also Driving)

By train. The Malaysian Railway is based in KL Sentral and offers an efficient rail service with reasonable fares across the country and to Thailand and Singapore. A railway line links Gemas to Tumpat in the northeastern state of Kelantan. In Sabah, a railway line links Kota Kinabalu to Tenom. The Kuala Lumpur-to-Singapore service is often fully booked. There is also an electric train service connecting Ipoh to KL Sentral. MYrapid runs KL's Light Rail Transit and the Monorail and riders pay by tokens for a single journey or pass cards for multiple travel.

• Electric Train Service: tel: 1-300 88 5862 (8.30am–9.30pm) or tel: 03-2267 1200 (7am–10pm); www.ets-train.com.my.

• Malaysian Railway: tel: 03-2267 1200; www.ktmb.com.my; book at https://intranet.ktmb.com.my/e-ticket/login.aspx.

• MyRapid: tel: 03-7885 2585; www.myrapid.com.my; LRT open Mon–Sat 6am–midnight, Sun and public holidays 6am–11.30pm; Monorail open 6am–11.50pm.

By bus. Buses ply the main towns. There are several companies, and tickets can be purchased at the generally very busy bus stations or online. It is best to book a day ahead. Mini-bus services are also available between popular destinations, and the fares are quite reasonable (RM10–30).

• First Coach: tel: 03-2287 3311; www.firstcoach.com.my; departs daily to Singapore 7.30am–8.30pm; every 2 hours.

• Plusliner: tel: 03-2272 1586; www.plusliner.com.my; departs daily 6.30am–midnight, hours vary according to destinations.

• Transnasional: tel: 1300-888 582; www.transnasional.com.my; departs daily to Penang 9am–11.59am; every 1–2 hours; hours vary according to destinations.

By plane. Malaysia Airlines, Berjaya Air, AirAsia and Firefly operate an extensive network of domestic flights to all major towns in Malaysia. MASwings services remote places in Sabah and Sarawak.

• AirAsia: tel: 03-2171 9222; www.airasia.com.

- Berjaya Air: tel: 2119 6616; www.berjaya-air.com.
- Firefly: tel: 03-7845 4543; www.fireflyz.com.my.
- Malaysia Airlines: tel: 03-7843 3000; www.malaysiaairlines.com.
- MASwings: tel: 03-7843 3000; www.maswings.com.my.

By boat. Regular ferry services are still in operation; the below are some of the most frequent. Note that trips can be cancelled or delayed if the weather is bad.

Mersing–Tioman Island (105 minutes): Bluewater Express; tel: 07-799 4811; departs 6.30am, 10–11am, noon, 2–3pm, 4.30pm, but guaranteed departure depends on the day's tides; RM70 return.

Lumut–Pangkor Island (15–20 minutes): Mesra Ferry and Duta Pangkor Ferry; tel: 05-683 5800; departs daily 7am–8.30pm, every 30 minutes from 8.15am; from RM10 to RM19 return.

From Kuala Perlis (45 minutes), Kuala Kedah (1.5 hours), Penang (3 hours) to Langkawi: Langkawi Ferry Services; www.langkawi-ferry.com. Kuala Perlis: tel: 04-985 2690; runs daily 7am and 7pm; RM18 one-way. Kuala Kedah: tel: 04-762 6295; runs daily 7am and 7pm; RM23 one-way. Penang: tel: 04-264 2088; runs daily at 8.15am via Payar Island and 8.30am; RM60 one-way.

Butterworth (mainland)–Penang Island (10–15 minutes): Penang Port Ferry; tel: 04-310 2377; runs daily 6am–9pm; RM1.40 per passenger RM7.70 per car).

Marang–Kapas Island (15 minutes): Suria Link Boat Services; mobile tel: 019-983 9454; departs daily 9am–5pm every two hours except Friday no departure at 1pm; RM40 return.

Kota Kinabalu–Labuan Island (3 hours): Labuan International Ferry Terminal (LIFT) services KK, Limbang, Lawas and Brunei; tel: 08-758 1006; twice daily from KK usually Mon–Fri 8am and 1.30pm, call to confirm departure; RM34 one-way.

Local transport. Taxis, mostly air-conditioned, are readily available and fares are metered, though in some places, like Penang, cabbies do not use the meter. In such places, negotiate the fare before boarding. In cities, taxis can be found at taxi stands or flagged down anywhere. The blue-coloured premier taxis, although plusher inside, are double the rate of a budget taxi. Flag fall for the latter is RM3, and every 115m (377ft) is 10 sen while a premium taxi's flag fall is RM4 and every 200m (656ft) is 20 sen. In Kuala Terengganu, Kota Bharu, George Town in Penang and Melaka, trishaws are a popular mode of transport for tourists and make for good photos. Rides within town limits range from RM3–30, depending on the distance.

Taxis (24 hours)

Ipoh 05-313 2375

Johor Comfort Radio Taxi, 07-332 2852

KL Public Cab, tel: 03-6259 2020; www.publiccab.com; Sunlight Taxi, tel: 03-9057 5757; www.sunlighttaxi.com.

Kuching: tel: 082-341 543

Langkawi Perkasa Taxi, tel: 04-731 7464; Pertek Taxi, 04-733 6843

Melaka tel: 06-334 6262

Penang CT Radio Taxi Service, tel: 04-229 9467; Island Taxi and Tours, tel: 04-226 6690

V

VISAS AND ENTRY REQUIREMENTS

To enter Malaysia, you need a passport valid for at least six months at the time of entry, with a valid visa, if required. Although Sabah and Sarawak are part of Malaysia, you need a passport to enter these East Malaysian states even if you are travelling from within the country.

Visa requirements. British, Irish and most Commonwealth citizens do not need a visa. Holders of US passports, for example, can enter Malaysia for three months without a visa. Always check the Immigration Department website (www.imi.gov.my) for details about formalities and visa requirements as conditions may change from time to time.

Warning: The trafficking of illegal drugs is a serious offence in Malaysia, and the penalty is death.

W

WEBSITES AND INTERNET ACCESS

News: www.thestar.com.my (The Star newspaper)

www.theborneopost.com (The Borneo Post newspaper, with a focus on Sabah and Sarawak)

www.klue.com.my (Weekly KL and Klang Valley guide)

Tourism: www.allmalaysia.info (Covers every aspect of Malaysian life)

www.sarawaktourism.com (Sarawak Tourism Board)

www.sabahtourism.com (Sabah Tourism Board)

Travel: www.seat61.com/Malaysia.htm (Information about rail travel in Malaysia)

www.myrapid.com.my (Public transport portal in KL and Penang)

www.met.gov.my (Tourist destination weather forecast; click on 'Amaran Cuaca' for English)

Cybercafés with broadband internet can be found in most tourist areas (with rates as low as RM2 per hour) but you can get wireless broadband (Wi-fi) free in cafés with the purchase of products. Some hotels provide complimentary Wi-fi either in the lobby or in guest rooms; others charge for it. Most major airports provide free Wi-fi as well. Prepaid internet starter packs are also available from major telecommunications providers such as Maxis, DiGi and Celcom.

Y

YOUTH HOSTELS

Hostelling International-Malaysia partners selected hotels to provide member accommodation in KL, Pulau Pangkor, Penang, Langkawi, Taman Negara, Melaka and Johor. Contact Hostelling International-Malaysia, 1–7 Block B, Impian Kota Apartment, Jalan Manau, off Jalan Kampung Attap, 50460 Kuala Lumpur, tel: 03- 2273 6870; www.hi-malaysia.org.my. YMCAs can be found in Kuala Lumpur, George Town and Ipoh.

Recommended Hotels

In major cities, Malaysian hotels can compete with the world's best and guests delight in the value offered. While resort islands manage to command consistently high rates, competition in KL keeps prices low.

The monsoon affects various parts of the country at different times of year, but inconsistent arrivals in recent years have made this unpredictable. Normally the arrival of the rains on the east coast, for example, drives rates down from October to April. Apart from Malaysian public and school holidays, the high season in Malaysia tends to be during the European winter (Dec to Jan) and Middle Eastern school holidays (June to mid-Sept). Langkawi and Penang hotels are normally full during this period and early bookings are essential. Don't come to KL during the Formula 1 in March expecting discounted rates.

Most hotels are rated by Tourism Malaysia from one to five stars. The only rooms visitors would want to stay in are those that are air-conditioned. All but small establishments charge 10 percent service charge and 6 percent government tax (the latter is not applicable in Langkawi). Rack rates displayed in hotels should always be used as a guide, and asking for promotional rates is recommended. Many guests shop around on the internet or use travel agents who can guarantee lower rates. Most hotels accept several credit cards.

$$$$	over US$120
$$$	US$80–120
$$	US$45–80
$	less than US$45

KUALA LUMPUR, SELANGOR AND PUTRAJAYA

Anggun Boutique Hotel $$$$ *7 & 9 Tengkat Tong Shin, Bukit Bintang, 50200 Kuala Lumpur; tel: 03-2145 8003; www.anggunkl.com.* Located in a pair of 1920s colonial houses, most of Anggun's cosy rooms and suites have four-poster beds and modern amenities. It is close to the shopping district and excellent restaurants, including

Sao Nam for Vietnamese cuisine, while the KL Hop-on Hop-off City Tour stop is opposite the hotel.

Bintang Warisan Hotel $$ *68 Jalan Bukit Bintang, 55100 Kuala Lumpur; tel: 03-2148 8111; www.bintangwarisan.com.* This centrally located 10-storey budget hotel is in the middle of all the lively Bukit Bintang action, just 100m (330ft) from the monorail station and close to Jalan Alor's food street. The busy lobby is forgotten once guests reach their comfortable and value-for-money rooms.

Carcosa Seri Negara $$$$ *Perdana Botanical Gardens, Persiaran Mahameru, 50480 Kuala Lumpur; tel: 03-2295 0888; www.shr.my/index.php/hotel-and-resorts/carcosa-seri-negara.* It's the preferred address of Queen Elizabeth II – she stayed here when last in Malaysia. The boutique property has suites that retain their heritage value while incorporating contemporary facilities such as internet. Dine on contemporary Malay fare in The Veranda or enjoy traditional English afternoon teas.

Putrajaya Shangri-La $$$ *Taman Putra Perdana, Presint 1, 62000 Putrajaya; tel: 03-8887 8888; www.shangri-la.com/kualalumpur/putrajaya shangrila.* This hilltop hotel is set in green surroundings yet has easy access to the administrative centre. Spacious rooms are tastefully decorated with a natural theme. There are complimentary shuttles to a shopping centre in Putrajaya, Cyberjaya and to Kuala Lumpur. Dine on contemporary Western cuisine at Azur or enjoy casual dining at the Palm Hill Café.

Sunway Resort Hotel & Spa $$$$ *Persiaran Lagoon, Bandar Sunway, 46150 Petaling Jaya, Selangor; tel: 03-7492 8000; kualalumpur.sun wayhotels.com.* This grandiose hotel is next to the Sunway Lagoon theme park, the country's most successful rehabilitated mining pond, as well as the Egyptian-themed Sunway Pyramid shopping centre, which has plenty of dining options.

Traders Hotel Kuala Lumpur $$$$ *Kuala Lumpur City Centre, 50088 Kuala Lumpur; tel: 03-2332 9888; www.shangri-la.com/kuala lumpur/traders.* Possibly the best value four-star hotel in KL is next door to the KL Convention Centre and KLCC. Choose park-view rooms and visit the SkyBar on the 33rd floor for KL's best evening vistas of the Twin Towers.

PERAK

Indulgence Restaurant and Living $$$$ *14 Jalan Raja Dihilir, 30350 Ipoh, Perak; tel: 05-255 7051; www.indulgencerestaurant.com.* Located near the Istana Raja Dihilir Ipoh, this luxurious hotel is in a colonial bungalow and surrounded by a landscaped garden. There are four rooms and three suites, each decorated according to themes such as Moroccan, English country, Italian and rococo.

CAMERON HIGHLANDS

Cameron Highlands Resort $$$$ *By the golf course, 39000 Tanah Rata, Cameron Highlands, Pahang; tel: 05-491 1100; www.cameronhighlandsresort.com.* Enjoy refined elegance in cool mountain air. This venue has been decorated along heritage lines but with contemporary facilities. Dine on Japanese cuisine in Gonbei or relax in the Spa Village.

Eight Mentigi Guest House $ *8 Jalan Mentigi, 39000 Tanah Rata, Cameron Highlands, Pahang; tel: 05-491 5988; www.eightmentigi.com.* Located just two-minutes from Maybank and off the main street in Tanah Rata town is this converted bungalow with tastefully decorated rooms and dormitory rooms with attached and shared bathrooms.

PENANG

Eastern & Oriental Hotel $$$$ *10 Lebuh Farquhar, 10200 Penang; tel: 04-222 2000; www.eohotels.com.* Possibly Malaysia's most celebrated heritage property dates from 1885, when it was considered 'the finest hotel east of the Suez'. All suites are spacious retreats. Enjoy drinks in Farquhar's Bar and dine on Western cuisine at 1885.

Hutton Lodge $ *17 Jalan Hutton, 10050 Penang; tel: 04-263 6003; www.huttonlodge.com.* In the heart of George Town, this budget hotel is in a heritage-conservation Indo-Malay bungalow, built in 1890. It's a 10-minute walk to the entertainment area of Chulia Street.

Shangri-La's Rasa Sayang Resort & Spa $$$$ *Batu Feringgi Beach, 1100 Penang; tel: 04-888 8888; www.shangri-la.com/penang/rasa sayangresort.* The 'Shang' is an institution among the beachfront re-sorts of Batu Feringgi. Relax in the Tibetan-inspired CHI, The Spa at Shangri-La or swim in the resort's two stunning pools.

Yeng Keng Hotel $$$ *362 Chulia Street, 10200 Penang; tel: 04-262 2177; www.yengkenghotel.com.* Located opposite the Ng Fook Thong Temple, this Anglo-Indian bungalow built in the mid-1880s was once a private residence but has been transformed into a 20-room hotel decorated with period-style furniture. You can choose either cosy rooms in the mansion or others that open out into an open courtyard and bamboo garden.

LANGKAWI

The Andaman $$$$ *Jalan Teluk Datai, 07000 Langkawi, Kedah; tel: 04-959 1088; www.theandaman.com.* This exclusive 186-room luxury resort in rainforest surroundings shares a pristine stretch of private beach with The Datai. It is also close to an 18-hole golf course (reopens mid-2013). A multi-award-winning spa perched on the hills overlooking the bay and a fun and educational Young Explorers' Club make this a perfect retreat for couples or families.

Azio Hotel & Residences $ *1-19, Jalan Pandak Mayah 7, Kuah, 07000 Langkawi, Kedah; tel: 04-969 8287; www.aziohotel.com.* This no-frills hotel, surrounded by duty-free shopping, offers flat-screen TVs and comfortable duvet bedding, at a budget price. Book in advance. A Muslim café next door and a Chinese food court around the corner offer many tasty choices.

Frangipani Langkawi Resort & Spa $$$ *Jalan Teluk Baru, Pantai Tengah, 07100 Langkawi, Kedah; tel: 04-952 0000; www.frangipani langkawi.com.* This resort has a strong environmental bias with green management practices in place and is ideal for those who want to commune with nature. Most rooms are in separate or twin chalets among tropical gardens within seconds of the beach. Sunsets from the beach bar are spectacular.

Malibest Resort $$ *Pantai Cenang, 07000 Langkawi, Kedah; tel: 04-955 8222; www.malibestresort.com.* The star attraction of these beachfront chalets is their great location, right on popular Cenang Beach. The chalets are clean and spacious, with comfortable bedding. Rooms are also available across the road.

PERLIS

T Hotel Kuala Perlis $ *45 Persiaran Putra Timur 1, 02000 Kuala Perlis, Perlis; tel: 04-985 3888; www.thotel.com.my.* Modern and chic, this hotel prides itself on offering good-value and secure accommodation (24-hour security and CCTV surveillance), just a 10-minute drive from Kangar town. You can opt for a day-use rate if you just want to freshen up before taking the nearby ferry to Langkawi.

KELANTAN, TERENGGANU AND PAHANG

Mutiara Taman Negara $$$ *Kuala Tahan, 27000 Jerantut, Pahang; tel: 09-266 3500; www.mutiarahotels.com.* This is the best resort here although it needs a little maintenance. It offers Malaysian-style wooden chalets with balconies, 110 rooms, dormitories and a nice camping ground with limited equipment for hire. Try the floating restaurants opposite the resort for more affordable choices.

Renaissance Kota Bharu Hotel $$$ *Kota Sri Mutiara, Jalan Yahya Petra, 15150 Kota Bharu, Kelantan; tel: 09-746 2233; www.marriott.com.* The city's only international hotel is within reach of the famous central market and state museum. There is a swimming pool and Chinese restaurant on-site.

Tanjong Jara Resort $$$$ *8th Mile, off Jalan Dungun, 23000 Dungun, Terengganu; tel: 09-845 1100; www.tanjongjararesort.com.* Tanjong Jara is an award-winning traditional Malay all-timber resort 13km (8 miles) north of Dungun on a 17-hectare (42-acre) site. There are 100 beach cottages and sea-facing hotel rooms (with great views from second-floor rooms), with 1.5km (1 mile) of private beach. The resort experience is completed by restaurants, two swimming pools and a spa village.

NEGERI SEMBILAN

The Royale Bintang Resort & Spa Seremban $$$ *Jalan Dato AS Dawood, 70100 Seremban, Negeri Sembilan; tel: 06-766 6666; www. royalebintang-seremban.com.* This four-star hotel in the Lake Garden district offers the usual comforts, plus a good Chinese restaurant, swimming pool and outdoor jacuzzi.

MELAKA

Discovery Café & Guesthouse $ *3 Jalan Bunga Raya, 75100 Melaka; tel: 06-292 5606; www.discovery-malacca.com.* Here you'll find single, double and triple fan-cooled and air-conditioned rooms and dormitories in a restored shophouse by the Melaka River, close to the main historic sights. A rooftop terrace offers scenic views and there are good Peranakan and Western meals in the café.

The Majestic Malacca $$$$ *188 Jalan Bunga Raya, 75100 Melaka; tel: 06-289 8000; www.majesticmalacca.com.* Fronting the Melaka River, this Straits- and neoclassical-styled mansion now houses the hotel's reception, bar and dining rooms, while the well-appointed rooms and spa are found in the adjacent building. Join the complimentary guided walk of historic Melaka and gain an insight into its living heritage.

Hotel Puri $$ *118 Jalan Tun Tan Cheng Lock, 75200 Melaka; tel: 06-282 5588; www.hotelpuri.com.* This carefully restored 1822 Peranakan house in the quaint 'Millionaires' Row' belonged to an eminent philanthropist. There are 50 rooms, a leafy beer garden and a spa.

JOHOR BAHRU

Thistle Johor Bahru $$$ *Jalan Sungai Chat, 80720 Johor Bahru, Johor; tel: 07-222 9234; www.thistle.com.* Formerly the Hyatt Regency, some of its rooms come with views of the Straits of Johor and Singapore. Facilities on offer include a two-tier swimming pool, a Roman spa, three restaurants, two bars and a fitness centre. It is within walking distance of town.

KUCHING

Hilton Kuching $$$ *1 Jalan Tunku Abdul Rahman, 93100 Kuching, Sarawak; tel: 082-223 888; www1.hilton.com.* Enjoy majestic views of the Sarawak River and the city's lively waterfront. Relax around the pool or in the fitness centre. Party in Senso bar or enjoy the club facilities in the executive lounge.

Telang Usan Hotel $ *Jalan Ban Hock, 93724 Kuching, Sarawak; tel: 082-415 588; www.telangusan.com.* This place is locally owned and operated by Orang Ulu people. Comfortable and well-appointed rooms offer great value for money. Dine on local Dayak cuisine, international dishes and Chinese food at two outlets in the hotel, located just 10 minutes' walk from Kuching's Waterfront.

MIRI

Dillenia Guest House $ *Lot 846 First Floor, Jalan Sida, 98100 Miri, Sarawak; tel: 085-434 204.* Located in downtown Miri and within walking distance of Imperial Mall, this family-run guesthouse is clean and comfortable. Double rooms and dorms with shared bathrooms are available but it is best to get rooms on the second floor as they are quieter.

Miri Marriott Resort & Spa $$$ *Jalan Temenggong Datuk Oyong Lawai, 98000 Miri, Sarawak; tel: 085-421 121; www.marriott.com/myymc.* The Marriott is the only five-star international hotel in this oil town. Located on the seafront but just minutes from town, it offers superior services and delightfully appointed rooms, mostly with sea views. Zest provides all-day dining. Relax in the Mandara Spa.

KOTA KINABALU

Hotel Eden54 $ *54 Jalan Gaya, 88000 Kota Kinabalu, Sabah; tel: 088-266054; www.eden54.com.* This hotel is centrally located in downtown KK and within walking distance of shops, restaurants and the ferry terminal for island-hopping. The hotel's concept is luxury living stripped down to its bare essentials. Note that rooms away from the reception area are quieter.

INDEX

Berlitz pocket guide

Malaysia

Twelfth Edition 2013

Written by Jack Altman
Updated by Hon Yuen Leong
Edited by Sarah Sweeney
Picture Editor: Tom Smyth
Series Editor: Tom Stainer
Production: Tynan Dean, Linton Donaldson
and Rebeka Ellam

All Rights Reserved
© 2013 Apa Publications (UK) Limited

Printed in China by CTPS

Berlitz Trademark Reg. U.S. Patent Office
and other countries. Marca Registrada.
Used under licence from the Berlitz
Investment Corporation

Photography credits: Alamy 116; Bigstock
1, 28; Dreamstime 4BC, 83; Fotolia 86; Hans
Hofer 18, 24; iStockphoto 2BR; James Tye/Apa
2TR&BL, 3TL, TR, CL, CR&BL, 4TL&TR, 5TL,
BC&BR, 6(all), 7(all), 8, 10, 13, 15, 17, 20, 30,
32, 34, 36, 37, 38, 39, 41, 42, 44, 49, 50, 52, 54,
58, 62, 64, 66, 68, 70, 72, 79, 80, 84, 93, 94, 97,
98, 103, 104, 106, 108, 110, 113, 120, 122, 124,
127, 130, 132, 134, 135, 136, 141, 143, 144, 147,
148, 152; John W. Ishii/Apa 23; Jon Santa Cruz/
Apa 2TL, 27, 47; Nikt Wong/Apa 150; Tourism
Malaysia 3BR, 4BL, 4/5B, 5TR, 43, 56, 60, 75, 76,
89, 90, 100, 115, 118, 129, 139

Cover picture: 4Corners Images

Every effort has been made to provide
accurate information in this publication,
but changes are inevitable. The publisher
cannot be responsible for any resulting
loss, inconvenience or injury.

Contact us

At Berlitz we strive to keep our guides as
accurate and up to date as possible, but if you
find anything that has changed, or if you have
any suggestions on ways to improve this guide,
then we would be delighted to hear from you.

Berlitz Publishing, PO Box 7910,
London SE1 1WE, England.
email: berlitz@apaguide.co.uk
www.insightguides.com/berlitz

Berlitz®

speaking your language

phrase book & dictionary
phrase book & CD

Available in: Arabic, Cantonese Chinese, Croatian, Czech, Danish, Dutch,
English*, Finnish*, French, German, Greek, Hebrew*, Hindi, Hungarian*,
Indonesian, Italian, Japanese, Korean, Latin American Spanish, Mandarin
Chinese, Mexican Spanish, Norwegian, Polish, Portuguese, Romanian*,
Russian, Spanish, Swedish, Thai, Turkish, Vietnamese

*Book only

www.berlitzpublishing.com